MANX*line*

Stan Basnett

Above: The **Monte Castillo** in Aznar Line livery arriving at Douglas in the Isle of Man for berthing trials prior to purchase at mid-day on Thursday 23rd December 1977. Note the two loading gantries visible both ends of the boat deck which were used for the self-discharge of refrigerated cargo over the side of the ship from the refrigerated hold below the car deck. These were removed later to reduce top hamper as they were not used by Manx Line.

Front cover: The **Manx Viking** in Manx Line ownership arriving at Douglas to commence her full roll-on roll-off service in August 1978 using the company's own linkspan on the Victoria Pier, some three months later than anticipated.

Back cover: The **Manx Viking** now in full Sealink livery and operating under the Sealink/Manx Line banner turning in the outer harbour at Douglas to take the evening sailing to Heysham in June 1983. The rear loading gantry has now been removed and two additional lifeboats have been fitted forward on the boat deck. The three legs emblem fitted at the Holyhead refit is clearly visible on the funnels.

All photographs by Stan Basnett

Ferry Publications, PO Box 33, Ramsey,
Isle of Man IM99 4LP

Tel: +44 (0) 1624 898445 Fax: +44 (0) 1624 898449

E-mail: ferrypubs@manx.net Website: www.ferrypubs.co.uk

Contents

Published by Ferry Publications Ltd
PO Box 33, Ramsey, Isle of Man,
British Isles, IM99 4LP
Tel: +44 (0) 1624 898445 Fax: +44 (0) 1624 898449
E Mail: ferrypubs@manx.net

Published: November 2006

The striking funnel logo painted on the **Lireco** when first on charter to Isle of Man Ferry Express, the forerunner of Ronagency (Shipping) Ltd.

Foreword

Little did I know when Bob Dearden approached me during the 1966 seamen's strike to form a consortium to bring goods to Island businesses, which were being seriously affected, that I would eventually become so deeply involved in shipping.

The venture which was started to meet our needs during the strike became very successful to the point where the move from using small coasters to something larger became inevitable.

The move to establish a full ro-ro service to meet the growth in our freight traffic was made and Manx Line was established.

I look back with immense pride on what was achieved and that against all odds we brought a true roll on roll off service to the Island and changed the method of transportation of goods and passengers for ever.

This then is the story of how it came about.

G.E.Duke OBE
Douglas, Isle of Man
November 2006

Geoff Duke OBE

The ship that made history - the **Manx Viking** outward bound from Heysham prior to the merger with the Steam Packet.

Introduction

It is not very often that work and pleasure come together but I count myself lucky that this has been the case throughout my life in very many ways.

Thanks to my grandfather, I have always been interested in ships and have had a particular interest in photographing all aspects of life associated with them. The Manx Line story is one particular event that falls into that category. My work within the Island's highway authority put me in very close contact with the movement of large and abnormal loads on the Island's roads at a time when the Isle of Man Vehicle Construction and Use Regulations were completely out of step with the rest of the UK, although it has to be said that many of the roads on the Island were just not up to the weights to which from the 1970s they were suddenly being subjected.

Later with the amalgamation of a number of works departments of the Island Government I became more closely involved with the maintenance of the harbours and also involved in the modernisation work, hence I enjoyed a privileged position from which to observe the progress of the new operation.

I started to write the story in 1999 after a chance meeting with one of Gerald Murtagh's sons which led me to speak to Bob Dearden and then to Geoff Duke whom I knew through my motorcycling activities. Gradually I felt that the story ought to be written as I had photographed much of the Manx Line's activities on the Island. For various reasons it was put on the back burner and now, seven years on, the opportunity has arisen for the story to be published.

I also knew personally many of those involved in the Manx Line venture. What has happened since is as a direct result of the determination and enthusiasm of those involved and this is in some way a tribute to what was at the time a very brave move. I do not think that anyone could have foreseen the impact it would have on the Island.

Stan Basnett
Glenvine
Isle of Man
November 2006

The **Lireco** leaving Douglas in April 1967 into the tail end of a south-westerly gale, showing the sort of conditions faced by the smaller coasters running the emerging container service.

Chapter 1 - The Embryo

Strikes do not always produce the end result sought by the protagonists. Human nature being what it is, entrepreneurs will seize the opportunity to create new business whilst the competition is shackled. This is the story of a shipping company born out of such a situation.

Intervention by the Labour Government of the day failed to settle a long-running dispute in the UK between shipping owners and the National Union of Seamen. The second week in May 1966 saw the threat of a strike become reality with virtually the whole of the British Merchant Navy withdrawing its labour with disastrous consequences on the economy of the British Isles.

The Isle of Man, like all islands, would be hit more noticeably, being dependent on sea communications for all of its goods and to a large extent for its tourist industry. The effect of the strike would be almost instantaneous and crippling.

The announcement that the strike had started came on Sunday 15th May 1966 and it was scheduled to begin at midnight. The Isle of Man Steam Packet Co. had been aware of

The Isle of Man Steam Packet Company's **Manx Maid** berthed at the north side of the King Edward Pier on 15th May 1966 loading cars that had participated in the National Hill Climb on the Island with the permission of the National Union of Seamen (NUS) who had declared a National Strike starting that day.

the impending strike for some time and had made arrangements for laying up vessels. Manx seamen were going to be hard-hit if the strike were to be a long one. The Steam Packet had ordered new tonnage in the form of another side-loading passenger car ferry and would be looking for the start of the tourist season to boost their income. A severe loss now could mean further fleet reductions to meet their financial commitments with consequent job losses. To the outsider it seemed as if no one in the industry was considering the long-term consequences of such action.

The Island, which depended on tourism for a large part of its income, feared the worst and the dreaded announcement came soon enough – the TT was to be cancelled! The National Hill Climb just survived but other events were to suffer. The local seamen employed by the Isle of Man Steam Packet Co. were well aware of the situation and agreed with the blessing of the NUS to meet a Sunday commitment for a Round the Island cruise already advertised locally with the car ferry *Ben-my-Chree*, which left at 14.30 and was full. The other commitment was for the *Manx Maid* to take cars participating in a hill climb event on the Island back to Liverpool. On completion of these sailings, both vessels went to Barrow to be laid up.

Tynwald, the Government of the Isle of Man, met on 17th May and was addressed by the Lieutenant Governor who pointed out the severe consequences that a prolonged strike would have on the Island. He proposed the formation of a Strike Emergency Committee with the objective of monitoring the effect of the strike on the Island and taking such action as was deemed necessary to secure the Island's survival. Tynwald endorsed the proposal and the Committee appointed comprised the Speaker and the Chairmen of the Finance, Airport and

This is the small Dutch coaster **Reiger** discharging general cargo at Peel breakwater during the period of the NUS strike.

The **Lireco** was the first vessel chartered by the Ronagency Shipping Company and at first was engaged importing bagged Polish cement for Island concrete products manufacturers. She is discharging at Castletown for Ronaldsway Brick Co.

Tourist Boards. Their first task was to secure essential supplies of fuel and food. The Committee held successful negotiations with the National Union of Seamen to allow 'mercy ships' to bring essential supplies to the Island. Steam Packet cargo vessels made several trips with food and other essential supplies and the Ramsey Steamship Co. brought in approved cargoes of coal for power and gas generation.

Tankers bringing petroleum products to the Island were largely foreign-registered and were not really affected by the strike but all fuel stocks diminished and the Government was forced to review levels of emergency stocks after the strike was over.

For almost a month prior to the strike the small Dutch coaster the *Zwaluw* had been running between Peel and Warrenpoint on charter to the Red Star Shipping Co. This company was formed by Gerald Murtagh and Bob Dearden initially to carry cement from Northern Ireland to the Isle of Man for Ronaldsway Brick Co. which was Murtagh's company. During the NUS strike Red Star continued to bring cement, food and agricultural machinery and were also exporting mica from the Manx Flux and Mica Co.Ltd. before being declared 'black' with local union workers refusing to unload the vessel. It was to no avail because the ship continued her regular run between Northern Ireland, Peel and Winsford in Cheshire throughout using non-union labour. To meet an increase in demand an additional small Dutch coaster the *Reiger* was chartered and made her last trip to Peel on 28th July 1966.

Cambrian Airways and British United Airways responded to a request for help from the Strike Emergency Committee and extra aircraft and flights were put on the Island routes. The competitors in the International Cycle Week were all flown from Blackpool in one day using chartered aircraft. By the end of the strike Ronaldsway Airport had moved 110,000 passengers and 1,600 tons of freight compared with 72,500 passengers and 360 tons of freight in the equivalent period during 1965. It would pave the way for the expansion of air traffic to the Island.

The deputy leader of the NUS, Tom Sutton, came to the Island on Monday 13th June to meet the local members and see for himself whether the strike was being broken by the mercy

As a result of business generated during the strike period the company built up a lift-on lift-off container service using Douglas as their Island port. The **Lireco** is entering the inner harbour at Douglas to shelter from easterly gales and passing the **Fenella** of the Isle of Man Steam Packet Co. Little did anyone realise that within a very short time the emerging company would soon have more than 50% of their cargo business.

The **Lireco** discharging at the crane berth on the Battery Pier at Douglas.

ships. He was treated to some of his own medicine whilst on the Island, being picketed by boarding house keepers, coach operators and taxi owners, and left the following day without incident.

We have jumped ahead, however, too far. The story is about Manx Line and it really starts with Bob Dearden, a young engineer, who came to the Island when he was 26 in 1948 as a qualified engineer taking contract work in the oil industry. He

The **Lireco** was put on the slip at Ramsey shipyard to have her centre mast removed and undergo her annual survey on 15th March 1967.

established Ronaldsway Airport Agencies Ltd. in the late 1960s, opened an office in Ronaldsway Airport and installed a telex. The object of the company was to handle air freight at Ronaldsway Airport and arrange delivery to the consignee.

His business inevitably overlapped on the movement of freight to the Island by sea and he soon found that the major importers of commodities to the Island were frustrated at the monopoly situation occupied by the Island's major carrier, the Isle of Man Steam Packet Co. He decided to do something about the situation. His idea was to obtain a controlling interest in the Company and he found that the huge shareholding was spread thinly in small parcels all over the world. Bob Dearden got seven people together and they agreed that they would all hold an equal amount of shares. He was no stranger to the Island having holidayed in Port St Mary, staying at the Bayqueen Hydro with his family, since 1933.

He set about involving a consortium of like-minded people to acquire sufficient shares in the Steam Packet Co. with a view to a take-over. Incredibly the consortium eventually amassed a 51% holding. Problems were anticipated with the Steam Packet Company but in the event the real problems came from within the consortium, there were disagreements and the coup came to nought.

Eventually the group, or what was left of it, out of the experience gained during the strike, saw that there was a business opportunity and formed a company styled 'the Isle of Man Ferry Express' in 1966. They decided to run an open-stowed freight service from Fleetwood and later from Glasson Dock at the head of the Lune estuary to the Island using chartered ships in direct competition with the Steam Packet. They sent telex messages from Bob Dearden's office to all the known suppliers to say that if they got their goods to Fleetwood they would find advantageous rates for carriage to the Island with discharge at Douglas or Castletown.

They had only been running for a couple of weeks when Bob Dearden received a call from John Edmundson of Walter

When the **Lireco** came to Ramsey for her annual survey she was by far the largest ship to be handled by the Ramsey shipyard since it had re-opened.

During the time that the **Lireco** was at Ramsey the **Pavonis**, another Dutch coaster, was chartered to run the service and is seen here entering Douglas with a full cargo of containers from Preston.

Edmundson (Haulage) Ltd. requesting a meeting which was duly held at Preston. It transpired that Edmundson's who had lost their haulage contract with the Bell Line - marketed as Bell Ferries - running between Preston and Warrenpoint, were looking for alternative business and were well aware of the activities of the new company, having been involved from the start with Ronaldsway Airport Agencies Ltd. The outcome of the meeting was that an agreement was reached with John Edmundson for Walter Edmundson Ltd and Ronaldsway Airport Agencies Ltd to merge - and form Ronagency (Shipping) Ltd, bringing together the expertise of both their companies. The Directors, all of whom put in £2,000, were Bob Dearden, Geoff Duke, Joe Bird, Dick Costain, Tom Wilkinson, John Counsell and Walter Edmundson whose son John was later to become Chairman.

It was agreed that the haulage would be handled in the UK by Walter Edmundson and in the Island by Ronagency. Edmundson's had a warehouse at Preston Dock and a berth was arranged with the dock master, but the dock company insisted that all cargo had to be containerised. Things moved quickly and Dearden took the train to Derby to a firm which had been manufacturing containers for the Atlantic Container Line, but had recently lost the contract. Twenty containers to ISO specification were obtained at £450 each which was the same rate quoted to ACL and these were picked up the following day by Edmundson's transport and taken to Preston. A number of Lancashire flats were obtained at the same time and within a week the new company was in business.

The first vessel that they chartered just towards the end of the National Union of Seamen's strike was the *Lireco* from Wagenborgs Scheepvaart N.V. of Rotterdam at £60 day. She

was a typical two-hatch Dutch coaster designed for general cargo and fitted with her own derricks on a central mast. By October 1966 the *Lireco* was running in direct competition with the Steam Packet operating a bi-weekly service discharging at Douglas on Mondays and Thursdays and making a serious impact. Early in 1967 the *Lireco* was due for annual survey and the owners wanted to take her to Rotterdam. In the event they were persuaded to have the survey done at Ramsey shipyard where she was slipped on 15th March. At the same time the mast, winches and derricks were removed and replaced with a small mast forward to allow the carriage of containers across the hatches.

The containers were all standard 20 ft containers dictated by the Isle of Man Road Traffic Regulations. The service ran between Preston and Douglas as the containers had to be lifted off at the Battery Pier using the 25-ton Cowans steam crane. The business took off in great style after the seamen's strike and the company at that time had 115 mixed containers in circulation. Some of the lucrative contracts they won included the shipment in containers of ejector seat parts from Martin Baker at Ronaldsway, furniture removals for local firm A.E.Corkill and supplies for Marks & Spencer. Another Dutch coaster the *Pavonis* was brought in on charter to cover the service during this period.

Through Tom Wilkinson's contacts with British Rail the opportunity arose to acquire a number of 720 cu.ft. wooden railway containers. The deal was done before the Isle of Man Ferry Express was re-constituted as Ronagency (Shipping) Ltd. As a consequence these containers which had been painted white to hide their former identity and to smarten them up carried the 'Isle of Man Ferry Express' logo. They continued to

> *"We opened an office in the airport and put a telex in there. We also found out that the people who controlled the input of goods into the Isle of Man were not people on the Island but companies in the UK who were shipping the goods and equipment. It was they who said whether or not the goods would be shipped by A or B.*
>
> *So with that telex we sent a message to all the suppliers of goods throughout the UK who were fed up at the time with shipping goods to the Isle of Man and some arriving and some not and the enormous amount of pilfering taking place.*
>
> *We formed a shipping company with Albert Hill styled the Red Star Shipping Co. and decided to operate between Fleetwood and Douglas. So we sent out all these telex messages saying send all your goods to Fleetwood. They started sending goods and we did a couple of trips from Fleetwood- one to Douglas and one to Castletown, all open stowed cargo."*
>
> Bob Dearden interviewed in September 1999

This is how the **Lireco** looked after her conversion with the centre mast removed and a new small foremast.

appear in traffic for years after the formation of Ronagency (Shipping).

Being dependent on the coal-fired steam crane and a berth adjacent to the sole tanker discharge for petroleum products to the Island created difficulties and so the company looked around for second-hand craneage and purchased a Butters derrick crane from the Forth Bridge construction site for £7,500. They negotiated a twenty-one year lease on part of the quay at Castletown harbour, erected the crane and moved the business to Castletown, setting up their office in the old lifeboat house in the outer harbour. The *Lireco* was doing three trips out of Preston every week but was idle at weekends and so a weekend service to Portaferry in Northern Ireland was inaugurated.

It was unfortunate that this coincided with the time that Preston was running down, and with the closure of the port a reality, Edmundson Ronagency moved their UK terminal to Glasson Dock which was operated by Walter Edmundson (Shipping) Ltd. Another Butters crane was acquired and erected at Glasson and the company was back in operation; other ships came on charter, sometimes discharging at Douglas as well as Castletown to meet the traffic demands. The impact on the Steam Packet was significant and led to them offering a competing lift-on/lift-off service, converting the *Peveril*, one of their cargo vessels, and changing to a fully containerised service.

The **Con Zelo** turning in the outer harbour at Douglas to return empty to Preston while the **Antarctica** awaits discharge.

Hull Gates' **Northgate** arriving at Castletown in January 1968 was the first unitised container vessel to be used by Ronagency and was the start of a long association between the two companies. Note the newly erected crane at their Castletown berth.

By this time Edmundson's had a controlling interest in Ronagency and Walter Edmundson was the Chairman of the company, but he never saw the completion of the move to Glasson before being succeeded by his son John. There is no doubt that without their involvement the company would not have developed as it did.

To keep up with the demand, Ronagency were very quickly

Hull Gates' **Parkesgate** being unloaded by the steam crane at Douglas in January 1973. The congested area at Douglas for marshalling is clearly illustrated.

forced to charter more vessels and right at the start the *Antarctica* and *Con Zelo* were on charter at the same time as the *Lireco*. In October 1967 a dock strike at Liverpool put even more cargo to the new company and saw the *Antarctica* return with the *A. Held* and the *Merizell* being brought on charter as well to cope with the extra traffic. The latter, from J. Tyrrell Ltd. of Arklow, was the first non-Dutch coaster to be used. In 1968 the *Lireco* went off charter, the service being run by the *Alderd L* and the *Kon Tiki*, joined later by the *Northgate* of Hull Gates Shipping Company Ltd. on long-term charter - the first fully unitised cargo vessel used by the company which now had by their reckoning 50% of the freight traffic to the Island.

In August 1969 the Ronagency Directors still looking for more ways to reduce costs chartered the *Tower Duchess* from the Tower Shipping Co. of London This vessel was classed as a barge, could operate with a three-man crew and an unmanned engine room with of course cost savings and she was also designed for container traffic. Both Hull Gates and Tower Shipping continued their association with Ronagency and the *Royalgate*, *Kingsgate*, *Tower Enterprise* and *Tower Marie* were to be seen on charter at various times.

In January 1973 the *Parkesgate*, which had been sponsored at her launch by John Edmundson's wife, was chartered from Hull Gates. She was also a fully unitised vessel but being too large for Castletown only ran into Douglas. At the same time the

"We had been operating about ten years as Ronagency and although we were making quite a reasonable profit we always had the problem with these small coasters and Castletown harbour operating in the winter with easterlies. We made a good profit in the summer and lost a bit in the winter, but overall we made a profit and we finished up with 60% of the total input of cargo to the Isle of Man and it was making its impression. But I realised early on that we had to look at a multi - purpose operation. It was something the Isle of Man needed - a ro-ro ship with the necessary facilities and I suggested this to the Board who immediately in effect said "pie in the sky" that's not something we can do. Nevertheless I was still keen to find some way of doing it.

This all lay in abeyance until such time as John Counsell, who was by then a Director because Edmundsons had become involved. John Counsell was John Edmundson's right hand man and he became a Director. He went up to Scotland on holiday and saw the Caledonian MacBrayne operations and the ships they operated with the hydraulic lift at the stern so that lorries could drive on and off. After seeing it he came back and thought it was a fantastic idea and just what we needed and suddenly the other Directors became enthusiastic about a multi-purpose operation.

We initially looked at the possibility of having a ship built. The idea being that it would be built on the Caledonian MacBrayne system if you like but built in such a way that at some future date she could be converted into a pure roll on - roll off vessel. We put this, by this time we had started talking to Roy MacDonald, to the Harbour Board but he - I can't remember exactly what he said - but something along the lines that they had been trying to persuade the Steam Packet to start a ro-ro service but that they weren't interested, which annoyed them very much. So he welcomed us with open arms when we went to him with the suggestion.

The question of having a ship built on the lines of the Caledonian MacBrayne ships was knocked on the head straight away. The Harbour Board wouldn't wear going through the walkway to get vehicles off the ship. There was no other way on the Victoria Pier of doing it. Roy MacDonald said, 'Oh you need a linkspan' and eventually it was agreed that the Government would build a roadway provided that we could find the finance for a linkspan."

Geoff Duke interviewed in September 1999

Northgate and *Heathergate* were also on charter. The *Susanne Scan* was on charter during February and March 1974 running to Castletown and Douglas covering for surveys. The *Wellowgate* replaced the *Heathergate* the following year with the *Wis*, another barge class vessel, coming on later that year.

Ronagency (Shipping) Ltd. trading as Edmundson Ronagency had been operating for about ten years and the company was making a reasonable profit. Winter gales severely disrupted the service being run by the 500-ton coasters required for access to Castletown harbour. It meant that during some winters the company incurred losses but overall they still stayed in profit.

The operation was so successful following the support from major suppliers that they soon achieved more than 50% of the goods traffic from the Steam Packet. Geoff Duke had suggested already that they should consider a multi-purpose ro-ro operation but Bob Dearden was opposed to the idea largely because of the limitations on commercial vehicle weights and lengths on the Island and their commitment to containerisation.

In the meantime the Edmundson Ronagency's service continued to be operated by the *Northgate* and Everard's *Celebrity* from 1976 until 1978. Much had been done through John Edmundson's involvement to develop the traffic with for

The **Susanne Scan** approaching the berth at Castletown in February 1974 was the largest vessel to enter the port up to that time. She was on charter to Hull Gates with an option to purchase.

Hull Gates eventually acquired the **Susanne Scan** and renamed her **Wellowgate:** by 25th April 1974 she was on charter to Ronagency and is seen discharging at Castletown. Her additional cargo capacity was being fully utilised, reflecting the growth of the company.

example agreements from Manchester Liners for door-to-door service from the Isle of Man to Canada, but as with all such businesses there was now a difference of opinion as to the direction in which the company should go.

The matter was put on the back burner until John Counsell saw the Caledonian MacBrayne service in operation whilst on holiday in the Western Isles. John Edmundson had a private pilot's licence and owned a Cessna 337 Skymaster which was operated for business purposes as Ronair. It was used extensively for moving personnel between the Island and the UK. With the question of ro-ro now a reality it was decided

Everard's **Capacity** was also a vessel used by the company from time to time. She is seen here at the Ronagency berth at Castletown awaiting empties for return to the UK.

that they would inspect the MacBrayne operation. Arrangements were made and John Edmundson and the IoM Freight Operations Manager flew up to Stornoway (Lewis) and met John Counsell and Geoff Duke there.

Enquiries were made to see what ships if any were available either for charter or purchase which might be suitable for a service between the Island and a UK port other than Liverpool. Further it was agreed, subject to co-operation from the Isle of Man Government for improvement to harbour facilities, that a new company should be formed with a view to creating a full ro-ro service to the Island to capitalise on the large amount of freight that they were now carrying.

In 1977 Geoff Duke and John Counsell approached T.W.Cain & Sons, a firm of advocates in Douglas, and details of a private company were drawn up and registered. The certificate of incorporation details the name of the company as Manx Line Ltd. with a share capital of 500,000 £1 shares. G.E.Duke, OBE and John Counsell are shown as the original nominee directors, the date of incorporation being 13th December 1977 and the registered office 13 St. George's Street, Douglas.

What had started as an opportunistic move to beat the 1966 NUS strike had now blossomed into a company threatening the Island's oldest shipping company and handling an ever increasing amount of freight traffic to and from the Island, and they realised that ro-ro was the only way forward.

Manx Line was born.

Chapter 2 - Ro-Ro Arrives

Directors of Ronagency were now involved in the new company and things started to move quickly. The bulk of the work in getting the job started fell on John Edmundson, Geoff Duke and John Counsell, the latter having to run the Edmundson side of the business in the UK as well. They were joined by Andrew Douglas early in 1978.

The problem now facing the Directors was the same one that had led to the Steam Packet building specialised car ferries with internal ramps and side loading. There were no linkspan facilities at Douglas nor at many of the ports to which they operated. The Directors through their Preston contacts were aware of developments at Heysham and the interest that P&O had in developing Irish traffic where the road traffic regulations were the same as the rest of the UK, unlike the limitations on bringing large and heavy articulated units to the Island.

Their biggest question was what type of ship to use. Should it be a purpose-built craft or chartered tonnage? Initially they looked at having a ship built using the MacBrayne principle but capable of conversion to conventional ro-ro at a later date when harbour infrastructure was in place.

By this time the company had started talks with the Isle of Man Harbour Board. In their very first meeting they were welcomed with open arms; the harbour authority had been in discussion with the IOM Steam Packet over the provision of a modern ro-ro service for some time and they had flatly rejected the idea. However, all was not good news because the harbour authority immediately rejected the idea of a side-loading vessel using the Victoria Pier as they would not accept the potential conflict of vehicles crossing the covered walkway which would still be used by passengers discharging from other vessels at the Victoria Pier.

Further meetings resulted in an eventual agreement with the Isle of Man Harbour Board whereby the Government would provide an access roadway from the existing King Edward Pier viaduct across the front of the Sea Terminal waiting hall and the new company would provide a linkspan to serve No 1 berth at the Victoria Pier. It was the harbour authority that insisted on the linkspan being located in this position following the recommendations contained in the 1972 report by the National Ports Council on the future development of Douglas harbour. The problem was that it took the roll- on roll-off recommendation out of context with the recommendation for

This aerial view of the **Monte Contes,** which was one of four identical vessels owned by the Aznar Line, clearly shows the large lifting gantries used for the self-loading of containers used for their refrigerated fruit and tomato traffic between the Canaries and the UK. These were to be removed from the **Monte Castillo** when she became the **Manx Viking**. (photo. Bryan Kennedy collection)

The **Monte Castillo** on her first arrival at Douglas on 23rd December 1977 to undertake berthing trials at the Victoria Pier prior to acceptance. This stern view shows the large rear door and ramp.

The **Monte Castillo**, now owned by Manx Line but not yet renamed, came to Douglas for the second time on 22nd March 1978 and is berthed at the Victoria Pier. The access road for the linkspan is well advanced.

the extension of the outer breakwater. As we shall see, this was to prove a costly mistake with disastrous results.

Much to the relief of the new company, the whole business had been carried on without the knowledge of the Steam Packet as they felt sure that had the 'cat been let out of the bag' the Steam Packet Company may very well have been able to 'scupper' the whole venture which was being promoted by the very people who had already won most of their freight business.

In the event the whole matter first became public at the sitting of Tynwald, the Island's Government, on 19th October 1977 when the Chairman of the Harbour Board, Roy MacDonald moved ...."that Tynwald is of the opinion that the IoM Harbour Board should proceed with plans to provide an approach road and pier-based facilities at Douglas harbour for a roll-on roll-off floating linkspan unit to be owned, installed and operated by an Island transport company who wish to open new daily passenger, car and freight facilities from a road/railhead at Heysham Harbour ....".

In the ensuing debate in which almost every member spoke the Chairman of the Harbour Board answered a number of pertinent questions referring to the National Ports Council report on several of issues principal among which was the fact that they had recommended the need to provide roll-on roll-off facilities. He went on to reassure members that the linkspan was being designed by MacGregor International and that they were a company that had provided 65% of all the systems used world-wide by car and freight ferries.

Reference was also made to the 1972 report in which the National Ports Council had forecast that within ten years vehicle arrivals could reach as many as 37,000 per annum by

The **Monte Castillo** departing for Leith on 24th March having undertaken more berthing trials which revealed some problems on what would be her regular berth with her draught of 16ft 6ins aft on spring tides. The lifting gantries which were to be removed at Leith are obvious.

The **Monte Castillo** turns as she leaves Douglas on 24th March and reveals her bulbous bow.

1981. He informed Tynwald Court that in the year April 1976 to April 1977 93,140 vehicles had arrived on the Island and that the arrivals April 1977 to September had already reached 75,519. When it came to formally moving the motion the Harbour Board Chairman in outlining the proposal commented ".....people will no doubt ask who are the company? What we have got is certain Directors of the Ronagency Company which has set an example of the container berth usage with other persons in the Isle of Man and the minute Tynwald says to us today go ahead they will form a new Manx company. Ronagency is still operating and will continue to operate...."

The motion was seconded by Dr. Mann and the resolution put and carried. The 'cat' was now very definitely 'out of the bag.' Clearly following lobbying from the Steam Packet moves were made by some members of Tynwald to defer progressing the harbour improvements on the grounds that the Government would find themselves providing a monopoly situation for a certain firm. This was put to the next sitting of Tynwald on 15th November 1977.

Those who are not familiar with the Island and its politics may find it hard to realise that an island with the population of a small town in the United Kingdom has its own Government within the British Isles and is not directly controlled by Westminster. Not only that but it is also an independent member of the Commonwealth Parliamentary Association.

The Island Government was a major shareholder in the IOM Steam Packet Company and Walter Gilbey, who was one of their Directors, was also a member of the House of Keys which is the elected house of Tynwald. It is no surprise then that the Steam Packet were prepared to go to any lengths to stop their rival, including trying to enlist the help of the UK Government, but they were too late.

Once again the Chairman of the Harbour Board had to defend the actions of his Board. In his response to members' questions he replied".....the Company that first proposed what

we have been proposing for a long time was the company that has been named today, Manx Line Ltd. Mr. Geoff Duke is in it, Mr Counsell is in it. There are two Directors and both Managing Directors, joint ... this company came forward with a scheme at their expense and people brought to show the scheme and to prove the scheme to our Board and every member of Tynwald was invited to attend...."

He could not resist pointing out that the two members who did not attend were the main opposition to the proposal. Once again it was put to the vote: the amendment failed and the Harbour Board was given the go-ahead for the improvements.

Now everyone knew about Manx Line.

At about the same time the company approached Captain Andrew Douglas, who at that time was with the Steam Packet Company, with a view to him becoming Marine Superintendent. A recruiting drive for senior officers was also mounted.

Manx Line now set about finding a suitable ro-ro vessel through their agents who found that the Spanish Aznar Line had two ships available for sale. The *Monte Carona* and the *Monte Castillo* had both been built for carrying fruit and tomatoes from the Canaries to the UK in the summer months before being transferred to their Balearic routes in the winter. The *Monte Castillo* made her maiden voyage on the service in 1976 and just one year later the service for which these ships had been specifically designed came to an end. She was one of four virtually identical vessels built for the Aznar Line and launched in 1975. The first was the *Monte Contes* followed by the *Monte Banderas*, the *Monte Carona* and the *Monte Cruceta* (which became

"....the DTI discovered that the whole of the car deck, which was refrigerated, was insulated with polyurethane which produces cyanide gas when it burns. No one else had picked this up and remember the ship had been surveyed twice and they hadn't found the engine problems or the polyurethane which presumably had been pumped into the cavity between the outer and inner skin of the hull as a liquid before solidifying. This of course contributed to the silent running of the ship as it absorbed all the engine noise. The DTI insisted that this all had to come out. You couldn't burn the plates to get to it and the only way we could get it out was with high-pressure hoses which was a very slow and painstaking job so that in itself delayed things.

Another thing that happened was that on the passenger deck on the port and starboard were two small cavities in which there was refrigeration plant - Andrew will remember it better than me - and even with the machinery out there was very little room in them. The dockers refused to go in and remove the polyurethane which virtually had to be scraped off. It ended up with Andrew doing the starboard side and me doing the port side. I think we were two or three days doing this and in a very confined space - bloody awful it was and it was not a very pleasant atmosphere either - but it was the only way to get it done.

I think I have been claustrophobic ever since....."

Geoff Duke interviewed in September 1999

Here we see the Manx Viking in Leith dockyard with work in progress. The forward gantry has already been removed and work has started on the alterations to the bow. Scaffold is in place for the application of the logos but as yet the name is not on the ship. *(photo. Peter Duke collection)*

the *Monte Castillo*). The earlier vessels, the *Monte Buitre* and *Monte Bustelo,* were the forerunners of the class with an identical hull form and engine layout but having a slightly smaller gross tonnage.

The *Monte Castillo* was launched as the *Monte Cruceta* in 1975 at the yard of S.A. Juliana Construction, Gijonesa for Naviera Aznar S.A. She was not commissioned until 1976 at which time she was renamed *Monte Castillo*. Having a length of 101.66 m overall and a beam of 17.10, she had two decks and a refrigerated hold below the car deck. The 2,753 gross ton vessel was powered by two 8,400 bhp 12-cylinder Atlantique-Pielstick PA6V engines which gave a service speed of 18 knots through two controllable-pitch propellers. She was also fitted with a bow-thrust unit.

The ships were owned by the Spanish National Shipping Co. which had received major funding through the Bank of Spain. They were available on attractive terms as both were anxious to recoup some of the capital expended on their construction. The vessels were still in service when Geoff Duke and Captain Douglas went to Newhaven to view the *Monte Castillo*. They were impressed with the standard of quiet comfort in the main

lounge which included air conditioning.

The deal was done.

Due to the limited availability of funds, the initial intention was to operate with a Spanish crew and under the Spanish flag as the vessel was virtually new and complete with a passenger certificate from the Spanish authorities. This idea was immediately rejected by the Unions and so the ship had to be re-registered and changed to the British flag which brought huge problems in its wake for the emerging company. Just to add to the problems, the Chairman of the Harbour Board had ideas of his own and insisted that the vessel should be capable of through loading. It is not clear why this was insisted upon but it meant that Manx Line had to have a bow door fitted to the ship. The consequence of all this was to add £200,000 to the start-up costs for the already cash-strapped company.

Meanwhile the Aznar Line were able to assist with financial arrangements for the £5m purchase of the ship and with funding in place Manx Line were in business. Thus far the new company had been operating from Ronagency's office in the old lifeboat house at Castletown. With the need for more space premises were acquired in St George's Street in Douglas and an office established together with a storage facility for ship's chandlery.

In due course Government funding became available for the harbour works and with the contract awarded to Taylor Woodrow who were the successful contractor, the first signs of activity were seen early in December. Manx Line meanwhile sought tenders for a linkspan and awarded the contract to MacGregor at New Ross near Dublin. It was the first ever order for a type F linkspan capable of taking a load of 115 tons and designed to withstand wave heights of 4.2 m.

The linkspan was designed by MacGregor and they engaged Newcastle University to build a model of the span and the harbour with wave information provided by the Harbour Board. The concern was the exposure of the position of the linkspan to easterly gales and following tests it was found that the span would be seriously affected as it was to be semi- buoyant as designed. The problem was overcome by incorporating a method of pulling the linkspan down onto the harbour bed in such situations.

It was constructed as a cellular box beam connected at the landward end to the roadway and with the other end supported by a buoyancy tank held in position by two chains anchored to the harbour bed and acting as columns under tension achieved by hydraulic rams integral within the structure. This was a simple engineering solution but more suited to an enclosed basin rather than an exposed position such as Douglas as was to be found to the company's cost.

The purchase of the ship was arranged subject to satisfactory berthing trials and suitability for service. The *Monte Castillo* arrived at Douglas on Thursday 23rd December 1977, while still in service with the Aznar Line, for berthing trials and was observed by many. The ship was resplendent in the Aznar Line livery and was a stern-loading vessel. Having successfully completed berthing trials to the satisfaction of the company and Harbour Master the ship left under the command of her Spanish

The linkspan arrived on 27th June 1978 having been brought from the Irish Republic by the tugs **Pullwell Victor** and **Dunheron**. The **Dunheron** is seen in the photograph positioning the linkspan the following day.

Captain and crew.

With the purchase complete, the ship made one more call at Douglas on 22nd March 1978 and left two days later for Edinburgh Independent Dry Dock Co. at Leith still under the command of her Spanish crew for alterations to be carried out to the bow section to provide a hydraulically-operated MacGregor bow visor and ramp. Additional work was also to be done to comply with DTI requirements for the transfer of the ship from the Spanish to the UK Register. The shipyard was chosen on the advice of London brokers, including Transocean Shipping, for the survey and work to be carried out to the satisfaction of the DTI. What the company did not know was that, due to industrial relations problems, the shipyard was then under threat of closure.

This was the start of a chapter of events which were to cost the new company dearly. The work was estimated to take twenty-six days but in the event it took sixteen weeks to complete. They later discovered that the shipyard was inexperienced in passenger craft work and that the *Monte Castillo* was the last job on their books. However, the manager of the shipyard informed John Edmundson that the ship would be ready for 18th May and all looked well for the lucrative TT period. Bookings were being taken with many of the motorcycle enthusiasts keen to support the company with their association with Geoff Duke.

The 1978 advertising brochure although modest had been in circulation from early in the year and aimed at the TT traffic which would give the company the much needed boost to their start in life. Heysham was marketed as being only eight miles from the M6, having good rail connections and ample car parking. The inaugural date was being given as 1st June 1978 based on the shipyard contract. They were offering full air conditioning and comfortable aircraft-style seating, two bars and a TV lounge with video screen, the first on any European ferry. They had designed special facilities for securing

The **Manx Viking** arriving at Douglas for the first time resplendent in her new livery in the early evening of 31st July 1978, but not yet in service and sailing with a temporary restricted certificate.

motorcycles and special discounted fares were being offered. Advanced bookings were rolling in and everything looked good.

The company were marketing their business aggressively and providing a totally different concept in travel to the Isle of Man from that of their main competitor. Passenger satisfaction surveys were introduced. Freight operators were being approached to see if the company could offer better facilities. A subtle point was the promoting of the service as a roll-on/roll-off service UK Mainland to Isle of Man, rather than the other way round. It was hoped that this might attract more business to the operation. The Marketing Manager was Peter Duke, one of Geoff Duke's sons, who joined the company in April 1978. His approach reflected his experience in the harsh world of marketing in the motor trade where he had previously been employed.

Heavy plant and equipment had arrived for Taylor Woodrow on the *Northgate* through Ronagency and been discharged at the Battery Pier while work on the columns to support the access road was proceeding to schedule on Circus Beach. The seaward end of the new roadway was completed from a three-legged jack-up platform. An hydraulic excavator on the platform excavated a hole in the harbour bed to receive the buoyancy tank and the anchor points for the chains which would secure the seaward end of the linkspan. This would enable the linkspan to be hauled down onto the harbour bed in the event of inshore gales which would result in rough weather in the outer harbour.

The roadway was completed on time. The linkspan, however, was not - its delay was due to construction problems and weather conditions for the tow. It eventually arrived from New Ross late at night on 27th June 1978 with the *Pullwell Victor* as the lead tug and the *Dunheron* as the stern tug. One end of the span was floating on its buoyancy tank and the free end wassupported on the barge *September*. The next day the linkspan was floated into position and the hinge section secured to the

baseplate which had been built in to the seaward end of the roadway.

Meanwhile, the *Monte Castillo* suffered numerous setbacks whilst in Leith. Insulation material, which had seemingly been acceptable to the Spanish authorities, was not acceptable to the DTI. The removal of the material destroyed much of the internal finishings. Some pieces of the bow door had been dropped in the dock allegedly deliberately. Geoff Duke and John Edmundson went up to Leith to see for themselves on 13th June and arrived behind the fire brigade who had been called to deal with a fire in a duct on the starboard side of the ship which added another £20,000 to the costs! The fire had been deep-seated and took four hours to extinguish. Captain Douglas and dock workers who had been on board tackling the fire prior to the arrival of the fire brigade were taken to hospital suffering from respiratory problems through smoke inhalation, the concern being the release of cyanide gas from the burning polyurethane insulation.

The ship had been surveyed twice prior to purchase and bought on the strength of those surveys. However, the DTI inspectorate discovered that the refrigerated hold below the car deck was insulated with polyurethane which had been injected between the hull and the hold as a liquid during construction and was now a solid insulation. Unfortunately in the event of a fire it would produce cyanide gas, as they had now discovered, and the DTI would not accept it, insisting on its removal which had to be done using water and high pressure hoses and adding further time and cost penalties.

Further insulation was discovered on both sides on the passenger deck level in two small plant rooms associated with the refrigeration equipment. The only way to remove it because of the presence of machinery and the confined space was to do so by hand. The dock workers refused. Out of frustration and seeing delays all the time Captain Douglas tackled one side and

Geoff Duke the other. Both agreed when asked about this that the conditions were awful and that it was extremely claustrophobic, something which had a lasting effect on Geoff Duke. There seemed to be no end to the problems of issuing a passenger certificate which in the eyes of the company did seem ridiculous for a virtually new ship.

The 18th May came and went and still the company had neither a ship nor a linkspan. The company had over quarter of a million pounds worth of pre-bookings which had helped to finance the work so far. It all had to be returned which did not exactly help the situation. It was devastating publicity and the Directors were understandably annoyed as all of their problems had occurred despite taking professional advice at each stage along the way!

Drastic action was needed and was taken. Captain Andrew Douglas had been standing by the work and the company were well informed of the problems. With the bow door now completed the decision was made that they would take the vessel regardless. With frustration at breaking point the company despatched a skeleton crew to Leith under Captain Ken Crellin, temporary closures were placed on unfinished work and the ship was taken out of Leith on Saturday 29th July.

With a temporary certificate of seaworthiness having been issued at the eleventh hour, mooring lines and other connections were cut, and the vessel moved to lock out of the basin without the knowledge of the shipyard. John Edmundson and Captain Douglas were at the lock gate when it was realised that although the ship now carried her new name there had been no formal naming ceremony. By chance John Edmundson had a bottle of champagne in his car and with a hastily provided heaving line lowered from the bow of the ship they secured the bottle and together performed a somewhat hasty impromptu naming ceremony!

The ship, now named *Manx Viking*, sailed round the north of Scotland to Douglas arriving on 31st July resplendent in her new blue and white livery. A large crowd gathered to see the new vessel arrive and the local press covered the event with enthusiasm. The ship arrived at the Victoria Pier bow in and connected to the linkspan with no problems. The visor opened and the ramp lowered, and always with an eye to publicity Geoff Duke rode off the ship on a motorcycle to the rapturous applause of the crowd. Berthing checks were carried out after which the ship left almost immediately for Heysham where outstanding work was undertaken by the ship's engineering staff and completed by sub contractors to the satisfaction of the DTI surveyors.

The *Manx Viking* entered service on 26th August. Now cash was really a problem and with litigation over the shipyard problems and disagreements among the Directors, it was a difficult time. More than two thousand people had made advance bookings for the TT and all that money, which had been spent, had somehow to be found and refunded.

During September 1978 the **Manx Viking** had the rear gantry and companionways removed by a local engineering contractor whilst berthed at weekends at the Victoria Pier.

Edmundson's and Ronagency had not completed their merger which was to be fundamental to the company's freight business and so Manx Line were initially totally reliant on Ronagency. Some of the original Directors were still on board although eventually Costain and Bird from the original Ronagency Board were to leave.

Keen to capitalise on the lucrative freight traffic won from the Steam Packet, the company now aggressively marketed their new ship to the commercial sector. It was agreed that Manx Transport Services (MTS) and Ronagency would handle the haulage side of the operation on the Island and that Walter Edmundson Haulage would handle the UK side of the freight business, much as had been the case when Ronagency Shipping and Walter Edmundson Shipping Ltd. had built up the Ronagency freight operation. The two companies continued to operate independently although to avoid confusion with existing clients the freight handling was marketed as Edmundson Ronagency.

From the outset the company made a conscious decision to provide four sailings a day throughout the working week. This proved particularly attractive to the multiple stores on the Island who now had a door-to-door daily service available to them with savings in warehousing costs and reduced dead stock. Marks & Spencer were the first to take advantage of this.

The down-side to the intensive use of their single ship was that it left little time for maintenance and the need for three crews to keep the ship in service for 24 hours every day. Another problem which soon manifested itself was the lack of provision for handicapped passengers. There was no lift from the car deck and there were no special toilet facilities.

The obvious external changes to the ship were that she now had a bow door and visor and the forward lifting gantry for containers fitted for the Canary Islands fruit and tomato traffic had been removed. Although charging half the fares and freight rates of the Steam Packet Company they were operating at a profit ignoring the looming problem of creditors. If they could continue like that they were confident they would pull through. Then disaster hit when the port engine failed in a big way with a broken crankshaft.

Manx Line could not operate their ship with passengers on one engine but they were allowed to operate a freight-only service. Keen to avoid losing their freight business this is what they did until the necessary spares were available for the repair work to be carried out at Heysham with the vessel out of service. During this period, further redundant top hamper in the form of companionways was removed from the boat deck by a local contractor J.D.Faulkner, who had also done work from time to time on the linkspan, at weekends and during periods when the vessel was at Douglas.

Manx Line by this time had moved their office to Viking House in Nelson Street in Douglas. Geoff Duke was the Managing Director at the Douglas end of the operation and John Counsell, still joint Managing Director, was based in Preston handling the UK end of the business. The company, however, were in dire financial straits: in fact they had been since early in the year due to loss of sailings through minor mechanical problems.

The overriding problems were cash flow and a series of capital repayments which took their toll on the company. Geoff Duke particularly felt the strain at this time as he was very personally involved attempting to keep the business viable and staving off creditors. The Midland Bank were no longer prepared to prop up the company without some security. He sold his motor factoring business to Quintin Hazel, sold personal shares to raise cash to pay creditors and was very near to personal bankruptcy along with Manx Line at this time.

Geoff Duke had a friend who was a manager with P&O and through him a meeting with the Chairman of P&O was arranged; it transpired that they were keen to be involved but in the event it came to nothing. Then out of the blue in October Geoff Duke received a telephone call from Mr. Eccles, the Chairman of James Fisher & Sons of Barrow. Through their presence at Heysham and the charter of their coasters they were well aware of what was happening and made a positive offer of help which was thankfully accepted. They acquired the whole of the share capital of Manx Line Ltd. Very soon after this, Fishers

found that the business was becoming too large for them and so subsequently sold 60% of the holding to Sealink.

Manx Line Ltd. was re-constituted with Geoff Duke as Managing Director with W.Eccles and J.F.Hornby of James Fisher & Sons. T.Wm. Cain and C.Q.Savage being the other nominee Directors. The shareholders were James Fisher & Sons (Isle of Man) Ltd. who now held 499,998 shares with T.Wm.Cain and C.Q.Savage holding one share each. The total debt of the company at this time was £3,932,020.

What is not clear, and was certainly not to the Directors of Manx Line at the time, was whether the approach from Fishers was simply a 'front' for Sealink. UK legislation at the time, in the form of the Transport Act 1962, barred Sealink from involvement with other companies and the assumption was that a deal had been struck with Fisher's to front the venture. Sealink had been trying to obtain a foothold in the Isle of Man for years but had always met with strong resistance from the Isle of Man Steam Packet Co. With Sealink now in the frame and with a greater resource available it became a different operation and at last with the technical resource that Fisher's and Sealink had at their disposal there would hopefully be an end to the mechanical problems that had dogged the ship for so long.

An announcement was made on 19th November 1978 that Sealink now had a 60% controlling interest and James Fisher a 40% interest in Manx Line. The company would immediately be re-styled Sealink (IOM). Captain Andrew Douglas who had been the Marine Superintendent with Manx Line since their inception now took on the role of Manager of the new company. Fred Cruxton remained as Commercial Manager at Heysham, otherwise the company continued to function as before. The Directors now were G.E.Duke as Chairman, J.F.Hornby of Fishers, G.Imlah from Sealink, J.E.Crellin and C.Q.Savage. With all of the advertising material for 1979 already in circulation the company continued to be marketed as Manx Line and in fact it was not until 1981 that this was changed to Sealink/Manx Line.

The last straw was the damage to the linkspan and the resulting further loss of revenue which would have crippled the company had it not been for the expertise and resource now available through the Sealink connection. However, the die was set, ro-ro would be here to stay and the Island would never be the same again. Daily deliveries from the UK were now a reality and small vans could arrive, deliver goods and depart the same day, avoiding overnight accommodation costs. Large items of plant and machinery could now arrive in one piece and the impact of heavy commercial traffic on the Island's infrastructure had started.

There would be no turning back.

> "It was absolutely traumatic," said Mr Duke. "I sold my motor factors' business to go 100 per cent into Manx Line and I was the biggest single shareholder. Yet at one stage I nearly lost everything I owned, including the roof over my head. I don't regret selling my business to go into the venture, but looking back I wouldn't want to go through the trauma of it all again. I think I've got so used to these disasters now, I just wonder - what next? In my racing career it was just the opposite, I've never been unlucky."
>
> The Guardian
> 16th May 1979

Chapter 3 - The Linkspan Disaster

riday 1st December 1978 started as a sunny day but with the wind coming from the south east and freshening. At midday there was a short troughing swell running across the harbour entrance at Douglas where the fetch on the sea was meeting the ebb from Douglas Bay.

At about 13.00 the *Manx Viking* came to within five miles of Douglas and was set for an entry but at the last minute turned south, headed away from the port and was riding the swell quite well. The intention was to wait and see if the sea state in Douglas harbour would abate and allow the vessel to berth as usual at the Victoria Pier linkspan.

By mid-afternoon the wind had backed to due east and increased in strength. The Steam Packet's *Lady of Mann* made a dramatic entry into the harbour and discharged all passengers and vehicles at the King Edward Pier and then left for the shelter of Peel in view of a worsening forecast.

Observation of the linkspan at the Victoria Pier revealed that the roadway was flexing almost 1.20 metres in a harmonic wave due to the swell running down the Pier. The hydraulic rams were unable to maintain tension on the chains securing the buoyancy tank to the harbour bed and the wave action was causing the tank to come up tight against the chains - this was inducing the shock wave in the cellular box beam. It seemed impossible that the structure could survive and in addition to the vertical movement it was also showing signs of sideways movement away from the Pier.

The linkspan had been designed so that in the event of excessive movement at the free end it could be tensioned down to rest on the harbour bed but in the event this did not happen

and it became clear that the hydraulic system could not cope with the loads imposed upon it.

The *Manx Viking* meanwhile arrived off Peel at 17.00 and sheltered to await an improvement at Douglas. With no improvement in Douglas the decision was made to discharge at Peel and Captain Dickinson brought the ship in at 20.00. Unusually the Chairman of the Harbour Board (Wing Commander Roy MacDonald) and the Secretary of the Board were on the pier with Geoff Duke, Captain Andrew Douglas and Guy Reid (the Office Manager) to meet her.

With the approach of high water at Douglas the situation with the linkspan had become considerably worse and shortly before midnight the inevitable happened. The linkspan broke from its connection to the approach road and partially capsized, having broken free from one of its seaward mooring chains which allowed it to sheer away from the Pier. This was to cause damage to the old ferry steps and part of the Sea Terminal building which it continued to batter as it moved back and forth due to the surge in the harbour. The noise of grinding steel and the wall of the waiting hall being hit was quite frightening.

Saturday morning revealed the true extent of the damage and attempts were made to secure the structure. The Laxey Towing Company's small harbour tug *Sunrush* received some damage whilst assisting in this work which involved passing mooring ropes across the harbour between the piers. Captain Douglas boarded the span at considerable personal risk in an endeavour to make it secure to avoid further damage either to it or Victoria Pier. Machinery was brought to the Pier and a

The **Manx Viking** was diverted to Peel on 1st December 1978 due to storm conditions at Douglas. She arrived mid-evening and discharged passengers although an abortive attempt was made to discharge cars by crane.

On the morning of 2nd December the damage to the linkspan at Douglas was there for all to see. It was free from its landward anchorage and the seaward end was secured by only one of its chains.

caterpillar tractor owned by Murtagh Plant Hire and a Poclain excavator made an unsuccessful attempt to pull the linkspan back towards the Pier. The fire service were also on the scene and an attempt was made to flood down the buoyancy tank.

As the day progressed, an examination of the seaward end of the approach road revealed that one of the end supporting piers had been completely demolished and the other severely damaged. The end beam to which the span was connected was also damaged but the hinge on which it pivoted was intact, the bottom of the linkspan deck having been torn away.

The morning Steam Packet car ferry *Lady of Mann* and the *Manx Viking* both sailed from Peel with the latter taking her vehicles back to Heysham as she had no means for vehicle discharge at Peel, somewhat vindicating the method of side loading preferred by the conservative approach of the Steam Packet to vehicle ferry operation.

During Saturday evening the fire brigade returned to the linkspan at Douglas to continue flooding down the buoyancy tank in an effort to sink the span onto the bed of the harbour and prevent any further damage. By 23.00 it had been righted and all seemed to be going according to plan. Then shortly after and without warning the span capsized onto its opposite side with the roadway now facing the pier. Obviously the amount of free water in the tank had reached a critical point with regard to its stability.

Further unsuccessful attempts were made to try and move the span using the *Sunrush* and the *Bounty* - a local fishing trawler. It was clear that the buoyancy tank was firmly on the harbour bed and refused to move but the end of the roadway

On Wednesday 24th January 1979 the salvage vessel **Moorsman** is alongside the linkspan displacing water from the buoyancy tank with compressed air when it became apparent that the unsupported roadway was buckling.

was still inherently buoyant rising and falling on the tide. Taylor Woodrow appeared on scene a week later, started work on an inspection of the roadway and carried out some temporary work to secure the end of the access roadway.

On 20th December, with the salvage contract awarded to United Towing Co., the tug *Guardsman* arrived at 21.30 with the purpose-built lifting barge *Moorsman* in tow. Continued easterly gales delayed any start on the work and the *Moorsman* was moved to the inner harbour assisted by the tug *Sunrush* to await an abatement in the weather. The weather continued from the east over the Christmas period.

Saturday 27th January and the linkspan has broken its back but is secured by the salvage crew on the harbour bed between the Victoria Pier and the King Edward Pier. Work on separating the two halves continued at low water with the **Moorsman** in attendance.

James Fisher's coaster the **Pool Fisher**, on charter to Manx Line, arriving at Douglas with a full load of containers during the time the linkspan was out of commission in an effort to maintain the freight traffic so recently won.

The **Eden Fisher** was also chartered during the period and is seen approaching the Battery Pier crane berth to offload containers. The two vessels maintained five return trips a week for unitised loads until the **Manx Viking** came back on service.

The intention was for United Towing to right the span, place it on a pontoon and tow it to the original manufacturers for repair. It sounded very simple but as with all salvage nothing went according to plan. United Towing were eventually able to commence salvage in the New Year under the supervision of their salvage master Captain Dennis Pierce. Salvage crews had been able to board the linkspan at low water and had flooded it down to allow work on fitting lifting lugs to proceed preparatory to the lift. All the salvage work was overseen by Mr. G.G.Griffiths and other marine surveyors from Casebourne & Turner of Liverpool who were acting for the insurers.

Having been delayed three times due to weather, Carmet's tug *Dunheron* arrived from Penrhyn on 12th January 1979 with the barge *Wimpey 73* carrying a jack-up platform and Andes crane for Taylor Woodrow. They were contracted to carry out permanent repairs to the approach viaduct which they had initially built. The four-legged work platform was assembled in the inner harbour at Douglas and the crane was loaded on board. The platform and crane were towed to the outer harbour on Wednesday 17th January by Laxey Towing's tug *Sunrush* and work commenced.

Later in the week the *Moorsman* moved down to the site to prepare for the righting lift as lifting lugs had now been put in place by divers. With the lift scheduled for Thursday 18th January the weather dealt another blow: easterly gales were forecast and with the weather worsening it became impossible to work on the span. The *Moorsman* assisted by the *Sunrush* made the shelter of the inner harbour with some difficulty.

The buoyancy tank had been partially pumped out and was almost lifting in the swell which was a point of concern as it was almost a week before work could resume due to the weather which remained from the east. The following Wednesday, the *Moorsman* was again able to connect airlines to

the linkspan and continue pumping air into the tank to displace the water, and by late evening it was partially righted.

However, the pounding on the harbour bed had created a hole in which the tank settled and this had the effect of leaving the roadway section of the span unsupported out of the water as the tide fell; by the afternoon of Friday 30th January a crack appeared in the side members of the box beam and then with the plates buckled it was apparent that the linkspan had broken its back.

Changes now had to be made as to how the salvage would be completed and it was a week before a further attempt was made to move the linkspan. The *Moorsman* was in position at low water with lifting tackle over her lifting horns and waiting for the tide to rise. In a snow storm the lift was under way by 19.00. At 20.00 the span had been righted and now free of its remaining mooring chain moved to a more secure location on Circus Beach.

Easterly gales continued to disrupt the work and the Steam Packet vessels were diverted to Peel on several occasions. Manx Line, anxious not to lose any of the freight business they had won, announced that they would continue to provide a conventional lift-on/lift-off service from Heysham to Douglas for unitised container traffic and Lancashire flats up to thirty feet in length which was basically the maximum permitted in the Isle of Man under the IoM Traffic Regulations. The announcement was made by Peter Duke, the company Marketing Manager and Geoff Quine who had been employed as Purser was put in charge of the lo-lo operation because of his previous knowledge of the freight business with Ronagency.

They chartered the 580-ton coaster *Celebrity* from F.T.Everard & Sons Ltd. for the service, advertising three round trips per week carrying 26 containers per sailing from 13th December 1978 until 3rd January 1979 after which five return trips a week would operate until the resumption of full ro-ro service.

To add more to the misfortune occurring to the company, UK haulage drivers were in dispute with the Haulage Association over pay and conditions and were threatening strike action; this escalated to a port blockade in the north west and Northern Ireland. Peter Duke was forced to announce that the lift-on/lift-off service being run by the *Celebrity* was likely to grind to a halt due to industrial action by the drivers. It was to affect the Steam Packet as well and the Island generally.

The strike was starting to affect the Island by the end of January. The *Celebrity* was sent to Eire for a consignment of 240 tons of foodstuffs arranged between the two Governments. Marks & Spencer were particularly hard-hit and had no frozen food in store. It was hoped that the strike would be short-lived and the *Celebrity* was scheduled to be the first ship to be loaded at Heysham on Friday 3rd February.

Following settlement of the dispute early in the New Year the larger *Eden Fisher* and later the *Pool Fisher*, both from James Fisher & Sons Ltd., were engaged to clear the backlog and maintain the service. Unloading at Douglas was done at the Battery Pier with the steam crane which had a lifting capacity of 25 tons.

Meanwhile the opportunity was taken to send the *Manx Viking* to Harland & Wolff at Belfast for dry-docking, survey and a further refit costing £1.2 m mostly to passenger facilities to increase the passenger carrying capacity to 800. More lighting was installed on the car deck, additional lashing points for commercial vehicles were fitted, a lighter mezzanine deck was installed, two additional lifeboats were added to the boat deck and a rubbing strake was provided to the hull. In addition an investigation into the cause of the problems with the port engine would be undertaken at the same time. The press release was upbeat for an April resumption of service and Fishers announced in their annual report that "Sealink UK Ltd. and ourselves are fully confident of the future of Manx Line Ltd".

1979 was designated Millennium Year by Tynwald to celebrate one thousand years of Island's Parliament. Numerous events were planned and the company were keen to get a piece of the action. The ship was repainted externally and internally whilst at Belfast. As ever with an eye on publicity, the opportunity was taken to name areas of the ship in honour of the ancient Kings of Mann. There was a King Olaf Lounge, a King Magnus Bar and a King Ivar Lounge with short biographies of the Kings reflecting the Island's connection with the Vikings and preparing passengers for their visit to the Island. The onboard shop was extended and the already state-of-the-art video TV system received a boost with the provision of a large screen. The ship herself carried a most appropriate name for the year. It promised to be busy.

The continued bad weather caused damage to the starboard Schottel drive unit of the *Moorsman* due to pounding on the harbour bed whilst working in the exposed outer harbour. After fifteen days of delay due to the bad weather, the *Moorsman* was

Late in February the salvage crew working from the **Moorsman** were successful in separating the linkspan into two halves and making each secure for passage by sea to the manufacturer for repair.

back on site. Over the weekend of 25th - 26th February 1979 the linkspan was cut in half and the roadway section floated free, later being towed by Laxey Towing into the inner harbour and beached at the head of the harbour. The other section with the buoyancy tank now watertight followed later. Temporary work was carried out to make them secure for the tow to Southern Ireland and repair by MacGregor. By the middle of March, United Towing had finished their work.

The tow to New Ross in Eire for the repair of the linkspan was delayed by continuing weather conditions as the tow was limited to a maximum of force 4 for a period of 48 hours by the insurers. The twin parts of the linkspan that had occupied the inner harbour were moved to the outer harbour by the *Sunrush* on Thursday 22nd March. The pontoon section was connected to the tug *Huskisson* of Alexandra Towing Co. Ltd. and the roadway section to the tug *Dunheron* of Carmet Towing Co. Ltd., leaving in the late afternoon. The tow was successfully completed the following day.

Meanwhile work continued on the repair of the approach road and with the amount of work still to be done the advertised resumption of service by the *Manx Viking* on 19th May 1979 seemed optimistic. Taylor Woodrow anxious to meet the projected date engaged another jack-up platform which was on site by the middle of the month. Despite the extra push the approach road was not repaired in time for the advertised resumption of Manx Line's services.

The *Manx Viking* came out of Belfast on time and first went to Heysham where the rest of the ship's livery was completed, once again at the forefront of technology. The ship's name and 10-metre-long company logo were preformed in Fascal 90 premium grade self adhesive vinyl. The name at the bow was applied in individual stuck-on letters 700 mm high and spaced over 8.5 metres. The choice of self-adhesive signing from the Wrexham firm was made over conventional sign writing in view of the complicated logo and the seven-year guarantee coupled with the fact that the schedule allowed little time for port maintenance.

Notwithstanding the fact that there was still no linkspan in place, the *Manx Viking* resumed the service discharging at the King Edward Pier with a service restricted to motorcycles and cars only, being loaded and unloaded at Douglas by crane from the after ramp of the vessel. By Saturday 26th May a temporary loading ramp was assembled at the King Edward Pier using one of Taylor Woodrow's jack-up platforms which was still on the Island and two Bailey bridges. The arrangement involved turning through 90° on the platform but the angle of the temporary spans was on occasion steep enough to cause damage to vehicles with long wheelbases.

In spite of all the problems, the *Manx Viking* was able to maintain a somewhat restricted service. Then to add insult to injury *Manx Viking* was out of service on Tuesday 29th May due to generator failure which was not repaired until the following Thursday when she arrived at Douglas with the afternoon sailing from Heysham. The sailing schedule was maintained through the high revenue-earning period of the TT, the only problem being traffic congestion on the King Edward Pier viaduct.

By the middle of June repairs had been completed to the end of the approach road; one noticeable difference was the provision of a steel gantry to hold the span to the pier and a double hinge to reduce lateral movement of the linkspan, with a chain to secure the landward end should it break again. The linkspan left New Ross on Tuesday 26th June and arrived at mid-day two days later under tow of the tug *Wallasey* before

The Queen and Prince Philip were present on the Island for the celebrations in connection with the Millennium of Tynwald in 1979. Manx Line were justifiably proud to convey the coach and horses of the Household Cavalry despite their linkspan not being in operation.

being assisted into position by the tug *Sunrush*.

The linkspan was connected on the afternoon tide and by 19.00 the span was in position and the supporting barge was removed. Manx Line were back in business again with a full ro-ro service two months later than they had hoped, again through no fault of their own. The enthusiasm and dedication of the staff at all levels throughout this difficult period had not waned and the company continued to run to schedule until September - the only problem being that any strong south-westerly weather was adding an hour to the passage time.

It was just as well because the Millennium celebrations were

The **Manx Viking** at the King Edward Pier discharging vehicles by means of a temporary ramp constructed from Taylor Woodrow's jack-up platform and two Bailey bridges. The photograph clearly shows the restricted space for turning between the two ramps and the steepness of the ramps.

The **Manx Viking** leaves Douglas in July 1979.

This general view of Douglas outer harbour in the summer of 1979 shows the shape of things to come with Manx Line's **Manx Viking** at the Victoria Pier providing a full ro-ro service - contrasting with the Steam Packet's **Manx Maid** which like all the side-loaders could only convey cars and small vans.

well advanced and bookings had been accepted from those anxious to be on the Island for the special events. The highlight recalled by former Purser Geoff Quine was when the *Manx Viking* carried "all the Queen's horses and all the Queen's men!" - 500 troops including the Household Cavalry and their horses, bandsmen from the 1st Battalion Scots Guards and the Band of the Junior Leaders Regiment who were conveyed to the Island for a week of military tattoos.

The climax was the visit of the Queen as Lord of Mann, accompanied by Prince Philip, to preside over Tynwald on 7th July at the ceremonial sitting and the Island's National Day. Her Majesty's coach and horses were also conveyed on the *Manx Viking* - something about which the company were justifiably proud.

Trailer caravans were not permitted on the Island but motor

Because Manx Line's berth at Douglas was still exposed to easterly gales the **Manx Viking** was once again at Peel on 6th October 1979 to discharge passengers only, illustrating the other side of the argument for side loading vessels.

caravans were and so the company embarked on a marketing exercise in conjunction with campsite owners to attract new business, height restrictions having previously effectively prohibited them.

The last of the plant and equipment used by Taylor Woodrow was removed from the jack-up platforms and they were secured together, being towed away by the *Dunheron* on 23rd July.

The usual arrival of winter gales started to play havoc once again as the linkspan was still exposed to the threat of easterly gales. The Saturday afternoon departure of the *Manx Viking* from Heysham on 6th October was delayed two hours due to there being too much movement on the linkspan at Douglas because of the swell caused by predominantly easterly wind. The *Manx Viking* was still unable to berth on arrival and was diverted to Peel, spending the night at anchor and entering Douglas the following day at 10.00.

Now with a greater degree of confidence, Manx Line renewed their efforts to win even more freight traffic and their latest brochure to the freight industry featured a Manx Transport Services vehicle unloading through the bow door of the *Manx Viking*. They stressed their modern approach and boasted the opportunities of exporting fresh Manx scallops to France and Belgium and oven-fresh cereals to Manx supermarkets! The brochure folded out to give comprehensive information to prospective freight operators with particular attention to the IoM Regulations which limited rigid vehicles to 10 metres and articulated vehicles to 13m but with a maximum gross weight of 26 tons. It also interestingly contained a useful 'at a glance' distance guide between Heysham and major ports and cities in the UK.

The company had now started trading as originally intended and hoped for a fair wind and no more problems.

Chapter 4 - The Take-over

One of the first things that Sealink did was to have their engineers inspect the linkspan arrangement at Douglas to see if anything could be done to avoid any repetition of the disaster in 1978. They came up with an idea to construct two concrete dolphins at the seaward end in which the linkspan would be allowed to slide vertically but any sideways movement would be restrained. On 11th October 1979 the tug *Dunheron* arrived yet again with a large crane and piling equipment on board to start work on the construction of the two concrete dolphins in which the free end of the linkspan would slide.

Easterly gales later in the month saw the linkspan once again setting up the harmonic wave action within the cellular box beam and various attempts at either releasing the tension on the chains or pulling the buoyancy tank down did not seem to make any difference. A local specialist welding firm were brought in to carry out some additional stiffening. This work continued through the night with some being done inside the linkspan.

On Tuesday 23rd October an announcement was made that the service would be suspended for a number of days whilst repairs were carried out to the hydraulic mechanism. The *Manx*

Viking, having been at anchor off Peel, sailed to Douglas early on the following morning and loaded by crane at the King Edward Pier. With the *Mona's Queen* also loading at the same pier, congestion was considerable. Eventually with loading complete, the *Manx Viking* left at 10.00, an hour after the Steam Packet vessel.

The company made strong representations to the harbour authorities that having been encouraged to set up a ro-ro service they were now being severely hampered by the lack of provision of proper protection to the outer harbour.

The following week work started on the building of the concrete dolphins, Norwest Holst being appointed as contractors. The *Manx Viking* resumed her normal winter schedule and all was well until November, when once again the vessel started to experience engine trouble which disrupted sailings. On Thursday 8th November the company announced that the *Manx Viking* would be going to Barrow on 11th November for repair and that a cargo-only service would resume on Sunday.

The advantage that the Sealink connection had now became apparent. With more resources to draw on, the *Dalriada* was brought in to maintain the lucrative freight service on which

During October 1979 Douglas harbour was subjected to a series of easterly gales which because of the exposed position of the linkspan disrupted the sailings of the **Manx Viking** which is seen backing out into an easterly swell across the harbour entrance.

The **Viking Victory** was one of two Townsend Thoresen vessels that covered for the **Manx Viking** during her annual survey. She is pictured here at Douglas.

Manx Line and Edmundson Ronagency were almost totally reliant. The ship was a Stena Line vessel on long-term charter to Sealink and managed by James Fisher.

The representations, the very public exposure of the problems in the harbour being experienced by the new service and the frustration of the travelling public must have had some effect as Tynwald, the Island's Government, approved a scheme for the extension of Douglas breakwater later in November.

Scheduled to reopen the full service on 3rd December 1979, the *Manx Viking* left Heysham on time but did not arrive at Douglas. She had broken down having lost power but could not enter Heysham Harbour due to a force 9 south-westerly gale and her lack of power. The vessel anchored in Heysham Lake and called for tug assistance. Eventually she was taken in tow by the two Liverpool tugs *Alfred* and *Crosby* and taken to Barrow where the passengers who had been on board for twenty-four hours were eventually landed.

Two days later the ship was back in service, the damage having been minor and caused by a burst water pipe flooding electrical control gear. The consequence, however, was the loss of control of one of the main engines and bow-thrusters which is why Captain Crellin had no alternative but to call for tug assistance in a force 9 SW. Alexandra Towing Co's tug *Crosby* took the head rope while the *Alfred* took the stern for the awkward entrance into Ramsden Dock which was achieved, but not without incident.

Early in January proposals to amend the Island's Vehicle Construction and Use Regulations to allow 32 tons gross vehicle weight became public. Immediately local conservation and nationalist groups were up in arms and demanded a public

An aerial view of the **Manx Viking** whilst she was in Ramsden Dock, Barrow during November 1979.

The **Dalriada** berthed at the Victoria Pier linkspan covering for the **Manx Viking** when she was at Barrow undergoing repair. The work is in progress on the construction of the concrete dolphins at the seaward end of the linkspan to restrict lateral movement.

The **Dalriada** backing out of Douglas on a fine winter's day on 11th November 1979, still covering for the **Manx Viking**.

meeting on the subject. It was left to Malcolm Corlett, the Surveyor General, to point out that the proposals would limit the length of articulated vehicles to 13 metres which would mean that the maximum length vehicles operating in the UK would still be restricted.

Peter Duke was once again drawn into the spotlight and set about outlining the company's views in a logical and reasonable manner. The objectors, however, were not interested in listening to argument about the economics of the issue.

For the company and the hauliers it meant that the situation was not much better than before as the maximum length container permitted into the Island was already 30 ft. Generally in the UK the 20ft ISO container was gradually being phased out and vehicle manufacturers were concentrating on producing 15 m vehicles to the maximum 45-ton weight. Any large vehicle coming to the Island had to move under police escort and be treated as an abnormal load.

Later the same month the Island experienced some of the worst weather for years. On Monday 17th December the wind reached hurricane force 12 westerly and no ships sailed. Later in the week, on Boxing Day, the *Manx Viking* suffered a minor fire and smoke damage in the bow thrust motor room forcing her to return to Douglas where the fire brigade were in attendance.

Once again the vessel was withdrawn from service and the *Dalriada* was back with a freight-only service. The *Manx Viking* returned within a week and continued on schedule until easterly gales at the end of January 1980 disrupted sailings

once again. Construction of the concrete dolphins had progressed and although there was a 1.5 m swell running down the Victoria Pier, the linkspan survived the battering - no doubt helped by the restraining presence of the new dolphins.

The second annual return submitted to the Companies Registry on 21st December 1979 fourteen days after the Annual General Meeting showed the Directors of Manx Line as G.E.Duke, J.F.Hornby, G.Imlah (Ports Manager, Sealink (UK) Ltd.), J.E.Crellin and C.Q.Savage. There was no change from the time of the effective take-over by Sealink.

The *Manx Viking* went for annual survey at the end of February 1980. On 28th the Thoresen ferry *Viking III* was brought in to maintain the winter service and proved to be a popular ship. Although smaller at 99.50 m, she was faster than the *Manx Viking* and made several trips in under three hours.

On Tuesday 18th March equinoxial easterly gales were forecast together with high tides. The *Viking III* arrived with the overnight sailing from Heysham, berthing at 05.05. Captain Douglas was in attendance and after consulting with the Master they agreed that there would be a considerable risk of the ship bottoming on the berth in view of the large tidal range. The vessel discharged and loaded what vehicles there were and went to sea to await the turn of the tide before reviewing the situation on the berth.

The weather worsened and the morning departure to Heysham with the *Viking III* was cancelled, the vessel leaving Douglas Bay for Heysham at 06.00. By noon there was a full

The **Ailsa Princess** arriving at Douglas on 2nd March 1993 whilst covering for the **Manx Viking**.

The Townsend Thoresen vessel **Viking III** arrived overnight on 28th February 1980 to take the morning sailing from Douglas covering for the **Manx Viking** which was off service for her annual survey. Slightly smaller in length than the **Manx Viking** the ship set a higher standard of comfort which proved popular with the travelling public.

easterly gale blowing and a predicted high tide of 10.3 m. The linkspan once again was taking a severe pounding with the tide overtopping the concrete dolphins. After the tide had turned the wind increased and backed ENE indicating a steady 37 knots with gusts to 47.

The seaward end of the linkspan was ranging two metres and then snatching the mooring chains once again with the linkspan bucking in what had now become a familiar whiplash effect with the centre of the span flexing between 600 and 900 mm - an altogether frightening sight. Andrew Douglas was once again on the span with the linkspan personnel trying to

secure it but was twice thrown off his feet, once very nearly through the side railings. The decision was made to withdraw but not before one of the operators fell down the starboard chain space, requiring his removal to hospital.

Later in the day Mr Keith Rowe, Fisher's Technical Superintendent, arrived together with representatives from MacGregor. With the weather moderating it was decided that the best course of action was to flood the centre buoyancy tank with 60 tons of water to dampen any further movement.

By 01.00 on Wednesday 19th, the swell down the Victoria Pier was averaging three metres and the ballasting did not

The **Viking III** was back again at the end of September 1980. Unusually for the time of year the ship was used for a Round the Island cruise on Sunday 5th October and proved extremely popular with entertainment being provided by the comedian Frank Carson and the weather!

To prove the point this is a view from the bridge of the **Viking III** as as she rounded the Calf of Man on the Round the Island trip. I heard no complaints and the ship was taken to heart by the Island. She also made some extremely fast passages between the Island and Heysham.

During the short period she was on service in October 1980 the **Viking III** had to contend with some particularly bad weather as seen here approaching Douglas.

The **Viking Victory** arriving at Douglas to provide cover for the **Manx Viking** also for a short period between 9th and 16th April 1981.

improve matters. During the morning Messrs T.R. Little representing the Salvage Association and J. Tomlinson of Casebourne & Turner arrived to inspect the linkspan that had surprisingly suffered relatively little damage although the hydraulic equipment had taken a severe battering. The span was passed fit for use and the *Viking III* resumed service the next day.

The service was interrupted over the next week whilst repairs were carried out, a new piston was obtained from Gothenburg and replaced in one of the rams. Clearly problems with the linkspan were not going away but obviously the concrete dolphins at the seaward end had saved the day.

The Steam Packet had sailed to and from Peel on 19th March as Douglas was untenable. The Manx Line service was back to normal from the 26th with the *Viking III* and the *Manx Viking* due back on service on 30th March.

At last Manx Line, albeit now with the strength of Fisher's and Sealink behind them, were able to cash in on the lucrative TT market which had eluded them for so long. Hard marketing campaigns resulted in the much-awaited traffic. Motorcyclists loyal to the name of Geoff Duke who was still

associated with the company flocked to Heysham. They were wooed by special discounts and the promise that their motorcycles would be supported in special frames and secured for the passage. Bike stickers issued with the tickets proclaimed 'tank not pumped out'. This was a side-swipe at the Steam Packet who still required motorcycle tanks to be pumped out before the machines were shipped as they were not secured other than by lashings and on their stands, something which had been a source of contention with the bikers for years.

The company then maintained their sailing schedule up to 20th July when yet again the *Manx Viking* was plagued by engine trouble, this time a dropped valve. Although temporary repairs were carried out it continued to lose odd sailings and a backlog of freight was cleared by Sealink's ro-ro freighters *Lagan Bridge* and *Lune Bridge* in the middle of July.

An upbeat press release was circulated in July to the Freight Trade which makes interesting reading and is included in its entirety as it contained a potted history of how the company came about and what their aims were for the future.

On 27th September the gremlins returned and the decision was made to withdraw the *Manx Viking* until the mechanical

Above left: Earlier in the year the **Lune Bridge**, pictured leaving Douglas and turning off the end of the Battery Pier, and the **Lagan Bridge** *(above right)* seen arriving at the Victoria Pier, were used to clear a backlog of freight traffic caused by the persistent mechanical problems referred to earlier.

Manx Line Limited: UK – Isle of Man Roll-On-Roll-Off Ferry Service.

. NEWS RELEASE .... NEWS RELEASE .... NEWS RELEASE .

Freight Trade Press Feature

If the Isle of Man economy is miniscule compared with that of big brother mainland Britain it is also by contrast extremely buoyant -- even booming -- with healthy annual surplusses reported with nonchalant regularity and a G.D.P. now exceeding £140 million.   In addition the real growth rate of the economy reached 13% in 1978/79.

Not bad for an Island population of only 64,000 -- and a powerful argument in favour of those who advocate partial regional independence from Centralised Government.

For, as is well known, the Isle of Man Government administers its own direct taxation policies, with indirect taxation the subject of agreement with the United Kingdom.

Over the years the advantages of the system have attracted many wealthy tax exiles.   They have also had the effect of encouraging an expanding commercial and industrial community and made the Island a prime target market for suppliers of consumer goods of all kinds.

This in turn has brought an urgent need for improved freighting links between the Isle of Man and the mainland.

Undoubtedly the biggest transformation in freighting during the past decade has been the switch from Lo-Lo to Ro-Ro, a process which began in 1968 with the introduction of the Island's first containerisation service by a new company set up by former world motor cycle racing champion, Geoff. Duke and several of his business associates.

This company, known as Ronagency (Shipping) Ltd., was the forerunner of the present day Manx Line.

For nearly ten years it operated chartered container vessels between Glasson Dock near Lancaster (later from Preston) and Castletown on the South West corner of the Island.

Before 1968 all non-bulk cargo was brought to the Island as open-stow or deck cargo.   Container ships meant faster delivery and greater efficiency.   They also all but eliminated damage to goods and pilferage in transit.

For further information contact:
Peter Duke, Manx Line Limited, Sea Terminal, Douglas, Isle of Man. Tel: Douglas (0624) 24241.

Continuation sheet 2...........

Within a couple of years, the Ronagency had claimed over 60% of freighting traffic to the Isle of Man.   By 1977 it was handling 8,600 container units per year.   But the next big step forward was just around the corner.   Geoff Duke and his partners had decided to go for a Ro-Ro service operating their own vessel and carrying passengers as well as freight.   They looked for a fully multi-purpose vessel capable of handling anything -- and found it in the 2,753 ton 'Monte Castillo' built in 1976 for the Aznar Line of Spain.

"We knew it was going to be expensive to buy and run," says Geoff. Duke, "but the beauty of a dual purpose ship was in being able to cater for two very different yet complimentary types of traffic and demand patterns.   In other words, passenger and private vehicle traffic would peak at weekends when freight, which favours mid-week movement, was at its lowest ebb".

Converting the re-named 'Manx Viking' into a luxury drive-through freighter ferry and installing facilities that would do justice to a cruise liner, certainly proved expensive, made even more so by constantly delayed delivery dates and alarmingly escalating shipyard costs.   By the time Manx Viking was ready for her maiden run under her new flag, £800,000 had been spent on her.

Installing Linkspan ship-to-shore installations at Douglas took a further £680,000.

All Ronagency business was transferred to the new company at the end of 1978.   By May last year Manx Line was operating smoothly and proving itself.

In the ensuing seven months, over 8,500 commercial vehicles were shipped by the new Ro-Ro service -- with Manx Line claiming a freight market share well in excess of 50% by year end.

The proportion is increasing all the time as the advantage of Ro-Ro in terms of greatly increased transit times -- cornflakes made at Kelloggs, Manchester, have been known to reach the shelves in I.O.M. stores still warm -- and greater reliability made possible by the all-weather capability of a large vessel, become more widely appreciated.

Manx Viking has virtually halved the crossing time to the Island compared with container delivery.   Turnround of the vessel on arrival can be impressively smart.   The current record for discharge and reload of 220 metres of freight plus up to 35 cars and passengers is only 30 minutes.

The opportunities introduced by the Manx Line Ro-Ro service have enabled Breeze Trading Limited, a Manx packer of sugar and coffee for British Airways, to operate to a 24 hour 'call-off' for deliveries to Heathrow, and compete successfully with London based companies.

The vessel will take vehicles up to 20' wide and is equipped to handle refrigerated transporters (they can be plugged into the ship's electrical system).   Livestock on the hoof can also be carried.

The Isle of Man herring and shell fish industries are benefitting considerably from being able to send refrigerated vehicles to the Continent direct from the Island.

Ro-Ro is also aiding the Ronaldsway Shoe Co., a major supplier of footwear to Marks and Spencer stores. Daily deliveries can now be made all over the UK.

Other big users of the new Manx Line Ro-Ro freight link include breweries -- Carlsberg, Bass Charrington and Harp all transport deliveries direct to the Island -- and distributors of foodstuffs. Manx Line now carries the lion's share of all fresh vegetables to and from the Island. Even some fresh vegetables from the Liverpool Market go via Heysham these days -- quite a feather in the cap of the new line.

For UK civil engineering firms, transport to and from the Island was always a major problem to be overcome when tendering for Manx business. However, Ro-Ro has undoubtedly eased the problem considerably. Transportation of all plant and materials for the £4 million Sulby reservoir project has been undertaken by Walter Edmundson (Haulage) Limited of Preston -- Manx Line's biggest freight customer. This major Manx Government project is to be followed by a £7 million harbour improvement scheme during the next five years.

For transport drivers, the Isle of Man run has become one of the most popular routes. The 3½ to 4-hour trip across the Irish Sea provides a refreshing break for them, an opportunity for some much needed relaxation in the very comfortable lounges on board which features deep padded high-back armchairs for every passenger, or the chance of catching up on a film on the ship's video TV system.

Passenger facilities and catering on the Manx Viking -- geared as they are to demanding Summer holiday traffic -- is first class and the subject of many letters of congratulations to the Line's management from passengers who recall very much more spartan crossings in days gone by.

Freight and passenger traffic for this year -- the second full season of operation -- is well up on 1979 and Manx Line confidently expect to top their target of 16,000 vehicle movements, representing two-thirds of the non-bulk cargo tonnage to the Island, by the end of 1980.

PD/EF - 3/7/80.

With the **Manx Viking** still out of service and the **Viking III** required elsewhere the **Antrim Princess** arrived at Douglas shortly after 13.00 on Wednesday 15th October for berthing trials, entered service the following day and stayed until 10th January 1981.

problems were sorted once and for all. It was the *Viking III* that came back on charter to maintain the service and managed to run a Round the Island cruise on Sunday 5th October which was well supported despite there being a south-westerly gale in force.

On Wednesday 8th October repairs and strengthening of the linkspan roadway which had been ongoing were completed and deflection tests carried out with an applied load of one hundred tons. The maximum deflection measured at the centre of the deck was only 17 mm. A week later, Stranraer's *Antrim Princess* arrived for berthing trials at the linkspan. The vessel entered service on Thursday 16th October and the following day Norwest Holst started preparatory work on the conversion of the linkspan from a semi-floating span to a conventional lifting span.

A revised sailing schedule was introduced for the winter

The **Antrim Princess** encountered east and north-easterly gales whilst on service and her sailing schedule was disrupted on several occasions. The ship was diverted to Peel on Sunday 2nd November arriving at 13.40 and discharged passengers only. All the vehicles went back to Heysham and were eventually unloaded at Douglas three days later.

The **Earl Godwin** arriving at Douglas on 25th March 1981 and covering part of the period while the **Manx Viking** was away for annual survey. She left the Island at the end of her service on 8th April.

period which included a double sailing on Sundays. No sooner had it been introduced than easterly gales caused more disruption. On 2nd November the *Antrim Princess* was diverted to Peel, discharged 135 passengers and lay there waiting for a moderation in the weather at Douglas to discharge the vehicles. In the event the ship left Peel at 15.00 and because of no change at Douglas she took the vehicles back to Heysham. Her return to Douglas was delayed a further couple of days due to a local dispute over manning with the National Union of Seamen.

During the period that the *Antrim Princess* was on service, some of the largest heavy plant and equipment the Island had ever witnessed arrived for the contractors Shepherd Hill for a new reservoir being constructed in the north of the Island. All the equipment arrived at once and was moved in convoy, presenting a unique sight and something that would have been impossible ten years earlier.

The re-organisation of the company into Sealink/Isle of Man continued: on 2nd October 1980 Geoff Duke, J.F.Hornby, G.Imlah and J.E.Crellin resigned as Directors and the following were appointed: M.S.Miller (Service Manager Sealink UK), Captain Andrew.Douglas (General Manager Manx Line) and C.Q.Savage who remained now as Assistant Company Secretary to G.Dick of Sealink. The company's registered office was now at the Sea Terminal, Douglas.

With the start of a new year and hopes for a better run of

luck, the *Manx Viking* arrived back in Douglas in the afternoon of Saturday 10th January 1981. At last the problem that had plagued the port engine had been discovered. Engineers had found that the engine bed-plate, which secured the engine to the hull, was out of line and this had imposed stresses on the crankshaft resulting in repeated failures. The *Antrim Princess* took the midnight sailing from Heysham and discharged early on Sunday morning, leaving almost immediately for Holyhead.

Conversion work was well advanced on the linkspan and the rams had arrived over the Christmas period. With all the thrust blocks completed the first ram was lifted in place on Thursday 22nd January 1981 at 18.00. The second followed shortly before midnight. Connecting the rams to the linkspan was delayed because of problems with the bushes which were remedied by the Isle of Man Railway workshops as they were the only people (other than the Steam Packet) having equipment capable of doing the work!

The rams were connected during Monday evening and completed by 02.30 on Tuesday. At 07.00, at low water, work on cutting the flotation tank free of the linkspan commenced and at 11.30 the span was lifted clear of the tank by the vertical rams. Laxey Towing Co's tug *Union* towed the tank away and the linkspan conversion was complete. Things were looking up.

The weather had been kind during the month but on Thursday 26th February a full easterly gale forced the Steam Packet to divert the *Manx Maid* with the afternoon arrival from

For a short period from the end of June to the beginning of July 1983 the **Villandry** was on service. She is seen in this photograph in Sealink livery turning in the outer harbour and taking the evening departure to Heysham.

Shortly before midnight on 22nd January 1981 Norwest Holst fitted the second hydraulic ram to the linkspan to complete the conversion of the span which would enable it to be lifted clear of the water when not in use.

Liverpool to Peel. Surprisingly, and maybe to prove a point, the _Manx Viking_ arrived at 17.15 under the command of Captain Woods, turned in the outer harbour and went astern onto the linkspan but kept the engines running during discharge, leaving immediately for the shelter of Fleshwick on the west coast.

The linkspan survived, was now able to be lifted clear when not in use and was no longer at the mercy of the unprotected harbour mouth. The irony was that it coincided with the start of work on the extension of the Douglas breakwater which was finished in 1983. Had the proposals for harbour improvements contained in the National Ports Council report of 1972, which had been commissioned by the Island's Government, been initiated immediately then this would have been a totally different story.

Chapter 5 - The End of the Line

Now with the full resources of Sealink behind them, the company were able further to expand their business, introducing many features which had not been available to passengers to and from the Isle of Man and no longer being dependent on one ship could draw on whatever was available from the parent company in the event of problems. Through bookings from the Isle of Man to the Continent were possible using British Rail connections from Heysham and cross-Channel services from Sealink.

Novel through coach traffic was being promoted but still fell foul of Isle of Man Public Service Regulations which allowed only foreign-registered coaches to operate on the Island but not UK - or Irish-registered coaches unless complying with special requirements which all seemed incomprehensible to the UK operators.

The impact on the Isle of Man Steam Packet Co.'s freight traffic was having a serious effect on their business. They had no alternative other than to commit to a freight ro-ro service themselves after having resisted the move for years for a mixture of financial, technical and political reasons.

In 1981 they chartered the *NF Jaguar* from the P&O Group. She was a freight-only vessel with limited driver accommodation but it was a move which would not have happened if it had not been for the activities of Manx Line. There was a certain irony about the involvement of James Fisher in the Isle of Man operations as in 1982 they had purchased the *NF Jaguar* from P&O after which date the Steam Packet were chartering her from Fisher's! In 1993 the vessel was purchased outright by the Steam Packet Company.

At the end of March 1981 the *Manx Viking* went for annual survey at Holyhead and the service was covered initially by the Channel Islands ferry *Earl Godwin* and then by Thoresen's *Viking Victory*. On 16th April, the *Manx Viking* came back on service resplendent in Sealink livery sporting red funnels with a three legs emblem in yellow. All was well until a problem was encountered with the new hydraulic rams which entailed the linkspan being locked off and the rams removed. Two days later the problem was fixed and the linkspan was back in operation in time for the 1981 TT traffic.

During 1983 the *Ailsa Princess* from Stranraer covered for the *Manx Viking* during annual survey and proved to be a popular vessel. There was no doubt that the company were also making inroads into the passenger traffic figures and the Steam Packet were not helped by industrial problems and poor passenger facilities at Liverpool.

The Isle of Man Fire Service had taken an early opportunity in 1980 to undertake a full-scale emergency exercise with the

Manx Viking as she was a new type of vessel to the Island and they were anxious to familiarise themselves with her. It was a timely precaution because in March 1983 there was a minor fire on the *Manx Viking* shortly after she left Douglas which entailed her returning to the Victoria Pier and a full-scale turnout of the emergency services. The fire had been contained by the crew and confined to motor wiring in the bow-thrust compartment.

During TT week 1983, Manx Line deck officers were despatched to Dover to bring the French-flagged ferry *Villandry* to the Island, having been brought there from Calais by a French crew. The ship was owned jointly by Sealink and SNCF and had been laid up for some time adjacent to a coal yard. She left Dover on 23rd June and arrived at Douglas later the same day. The vessel stayed on service until 10th July.

By June 1983 the Directors of the company were Captain A.C.Douglas (General Manager), M.S.Miller and C.Q.Savage. The share capital still showed at £500,000 but the debt was now declared at £11,911,811 reflecting the cost to the company of the linkspan disaster.

In July 1984 the British Government announced that they had concluded a deal to sell Sealink to Sea Containers which resulted in Heysham and Manx Line coming under the Sea Containers banner. This brought James Sherwood, the President of Sea Containers, to the Isle of Man to see for himself the

During the **Manx Viking**'s annual survey at Holyhead in 1981, three-legged emblems painted yellow were fixed to the funnels. The ship emerged in full Sealink colours on 16th April. (photo. Capt. Roger Moore)

A full turn-out of the IOM Fire Service to the **Manx Viking** which had returned to Douglas following what turned out to be a minor fire in the bow thrust motor room. The ship was later able to resume passage to Heysham.

Sealink/Manx Line operation.

By September the cumulative effect of the Manx Line operation on the Isle of Man Steam Packet Co. had reached serious proportions. Professional advice was sought from leading accountants and amongst the options presented was a proposal to merge.

The Steam Packet meanwhile had now belatedly committed

An engine room view on the **Manx Viking** showing one bank of cylinders of one of the vee twelve cylinder Pielstick PA6V engines which powered the ship.

to commencing a full ro-ro service themselves. Merger talks had started and Sea Containers aware of their dilemma offered the *Villandry* as a suitable vessel. Instead they chose the *Tamira*, formerly Townsend's *Free Enterprise III*, which they purchased from the Mira Shipping Line in 1984 - a choice they were to regret.

In the meantime negotiations for the merger continued with offer and counter-offer dragging on into 1985 and coming to a head on 1st February 1985. A press conference was held at Imperial Buildings, the office of the IOM Steam Packet Company, and an announcement made that Sealink/Manx Line and the Isle of Man Steam Packet would merge with Sea Containers taking a 40% shareholding. There would be four Directors from each company.

There was a huge reaction from the Steam Packet shareholders and a group opposed to the merger eventually got together but with only 11% of the shareholding were unable to be effective. However there was to be an ironic twist to this tale when at 08.00 on Friday 29th March 1986 it was announced that Jim Sherwood of Sea Containers had achieved what Bob Dearden had hoped for thirty years or so earlier when he acquired 58% of the shares of the IOM Steam Packet Co.

Later the same year the decision was made to dispose of the *Manx Viking* which by that time was considered to be too slow for the service. The ship made her last voyage from Douglas on 29th September 1986 and some days later left Heysham for Barrow to be laid up awaiting sale.

The last tangible link with Manx Line had gone.

One long-term ambition of the Manx Line company had

A superb picture of the **Manx Viking**, now in full IOM Steam Packet ownership and livery, departing Heysham for Douglas on Friday, 6th June 19
(photo. Bryan Kennedy)

The **Skudenes** formerly the **Manx Viking** taken at the berth at Mekjarvik, which is the ferry terminal at Stavanger for the sailings to the north of the country. (photo. Capt Ken Crellin collection)

The **Manx Viking** now as the **Nindawayma** lies at Les Mecins, Quebec in a somewhat neglected state awaiting an uncertain future. (photo. Richard Seville)

been to revolutionise sea travel by introducing a fast craft service on the route. They went as far as setting up another company to explore the feasibility. Hoverlink was established with an office in Finch Road, Douglas. It came to nought as events overtook them.

However, Manx Line Ltd still lingered in the background and continued to function as a ghost of its former self to deal with outstanding creditors and other matters which still had to be resolved such as the insurance claim in respect of the linkspan. The annual return for 1985 still declared the share capital as £500,000 and the major shareholder as Manx Line Holdings Ltd. The debt of the company had, however, reduced to £9,169,678.

The Directors now were L.C. Merryweather, OBE, R.Holmes (both Directors of Sealink UK Ltd. and Manx Line Holdings), J.E.Crellin, P.G.Crellin and C.Q.Savage of Cains and Captain A.C.Douglas. A number of changes took place over the following years but always with a Sealink presence. W.Henderson, who had succeeded L.C.Merryweather, resigned in April 1988 as did Captain Douglas leaving J.E.Crellin, P.G.Crellin and C.Q.Savage of Cains and M.A.Phelps (Personnel Director, Sealink UK) as holding Directors leading to the winding-up of the company.

Now with the insurance claim for the damaged linkspan, which was in the region of £10m, settled after protracted negotiation Deloitte & Touche were appointed liquidators and the company was declared solvent and wound up on 3rd April 2000. The assets of £9,919 were distributed to the

When the **Manx Viking** celebrated her 1,000 sailing on 20th February 1980 Sealink/Manx Line were quick to make the most of the event. 'Viking maidens' were included in the publicity for the media and here they are with Captain Michael Leadley on the bridge of the ship at Heysham. (photo. Peter Duke collection)

The cafeteria service on the **Manx Viking** was a novel introduction to travel on the Isle of Man routes and contrasted sharply with the silver service offered by their rival. Manx Line made much of the service offered in their publicity material. (photo. Peter Duke collection)

Captain Crellin on the wing of the **Manx Viking** manoeuvres the vessel astern in the tight confines of Heysham harbour using the combinators, giving him complete instant control over the ship by way of the variable pitch propellers. (photo. Capt Ken Crellin collection)

shareholders.

The subsequent fate of the *Manx Viking* makes for an interesting end to the story. After being in service with the Steam Packet she was duly sold to Det Stavangerske Dampskibsselskab of Stavanger, Norway for service in Stavanger Fjord between Stavanger and Skudeneshavn and named *Manx* for the delivery voyage. Renamed *Skudenes*, she re-entered service but after a year was being offered for sale yet again.

Bought by Ontario Northland Marine Services in March 1989 she was named *Ontario No1* for delivery across the Atlantic to Shelbourne, Nova Scotia for a refit. On 4th May, as soon as conditions in the St Lawrence Seaway permitted, she left for Owen Sound via the Great Lakes to take up her new service on Lake Huron.

Now renamed *Nindawayma* (an Ojibway Indian word

meaning 'little sister') she operated on the Tobermory and South Baymouth service until being withdrawn in 1992 and laid up at Owen Sound having failed to build up the traffic on the route as a running mate to the *Chi-Cheemaun.*

After eight years lying idle the ship was bought by the Verreault Marine & Navigation Services Co. for $C1.5 m. in November 2000. The *Nindawayma* was towed from Owen Sound by the tug *Point Carroll* and was met in lower Lake Huron by the tug *Menasha* for assistance through the St Clair and Detroit rivers. The tow continued through Lake Erie to Port Colborne where another tug assisted the *Point Carroll* through the Welland Canal and the Seaway.

On arrival at Quebec she was delivered to Les Mecins yard and there languishes to the present day. Ideas for conversion to a cable ship and to a floating casino have come to nought.

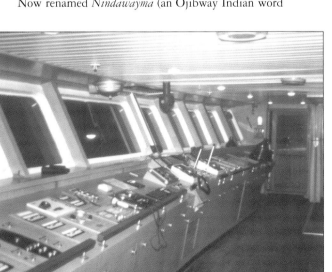

This photograph of the bridge of the **Manx Viking** was taken at night at Peel on the night of the linkspan failure. It was extremely modern and comfortable by comparison with the bridge facilities navigating officers had on the early Steam Packet side-loaders.

The engine control room of the **Manx Viking** offered a soundproof environment for the duty engineer to monitor and control all the engine room propulsion machinery and electrical generating equipment.

Chapter 6 - The Personnel

The story of Manx Line would not be complete without reference to the staff employed by the company who, against all odds, stood by its ideals.

Once the Chairman of the Harbour Board announced in Tynwald the name of the new shipping company and the names of the joint Managing Directors, the 'cat was out of the bag' and recruitment of staff started in earnest.

Captain Andrew Douglas had already been approached by Guy Reid, Geoff Duke's brother-in-law, about the post of Marine Superintendent in November 1977. He was appointed in January 1978 and at the time he was a navigating officer with the IOM Steam Packet Company. As a young man with a long family tradition in the Steam Packet, it must have been a brave decision for him to make.

Many young local men who qualified for a career at sea and eventually married and took on family and financial commitments looked to the Steam Packet for security and the advantage of operating out of their home port with the chance of more time at home. The down-side was that promotion prospects were long term and often a case of waiting for 'dead men's shoes'.

Andrew Douglas was the first employee for Manx Line beyond the Directors and was no exception to this. Trained at HMS Conway Sea Training School he was no doubt tempted by the prospect of becoming Marine Superintendent of the new company which he might have achieved in the Steam Packet in thirty years' time with more than a bit of luck!

Advertisements were placed in the local press and the nautical journals. Other Steam Packet personnel were attracted by the rates and terms of employment, perhaps the most attractive of which was two weeks on and one week off duty. This was necessitated by the proposed sailing schedule of 28 sailings each week in the summer months and 18 during the winter.

Applications started rolling in. Ironically many applicants were being interviewed by their former colleague. The first navigating officer to be appointed was Captain R.M. Dickinson on 24th April 1978 taking one of the three posts of Master of the new ship. He was also Conway trained and was a Master with the Steam Packet originally with the *Conister* and latterly the *Snaefell*. He was followed by Captain. J.W. Woods in May who had been with the Steam Packet earlier in his career but returned to Manx Line from deep sea. The third Captain for the three watch system required by the company was Captain T.K. Crellin who also joined later in May 1978, relinquishing command of the Steam Packet vessel *Conister*.

Strangely, nearly all the navigating officers were from the Island whereas the engineering staff were drawn from further afield although some had Manx connections. This perhaps reflected the different ethos between the two disciplines - whereas each ship is different all the engines are fundamentally the same! Frank O'Neill for example although born on the Island had decided upon a career in engineering at sea and had a position with Cunard. Just like the navigating officers it was a brave move to leave a secure job for Manx Line. The examples quoted are from those to whom I have personally spoken and are representative of pretty well all those who were employed at the outset.

The celebrations of the 1,000 sailing included an onboard reception for company officials and local dignitaries. Seen left to right are Captain Ken Crellin, George Imlah (Director), Mrs I Welldrake (Mayor of Lancaster), Geoff Duke (Chairman of Manx Line), John Hornby (Director) and Peter Duke (Marketing Manager). *(photo. Peter Duke collection)*

Members of the catering staff display their fayre and await the guests for the same occasion. *(photo. Peter Duke collection)*

The final Manx Line annual staff dinner at the Empress Hotel in Douglas. *Bottom row left to right:* Chris Kneale, Geoff Shimmin, Fred Cuxton, Tony Temple, Vincent Bowe, *First row left to right:* Billy Magee, Rose Leonard, Fred Adlam, Linda Corlett, Amber Brennan, Bernadette Crossley, Angie Kinley, June Collister, not identified, Dave Kelso, Roger Moore. *Second row left to right:* Frank Smoker, Peter Duke, Frank O'Neil, Andrew Douglas, John Edmundson, Andy Westran. *Third row left to right:* Ray Dickinson, Jack Woods, Peter Reid, Chris Smethurst, John Molyneux, Roger Jackson. *Top row left to right:* Ken Crellin, John Fitton, Les Moreland, Geoff Quine, Ewan Faragher, Don Meyrick.

Geoff Quine was something of an exception as he had not been to sea but had been heavily involved with Ronagency on the haulage side. He applied for the position of Purser and was successful. At the age of 56 he was the oldest member of the crew and started what was in effect a new career, being thrown in at the deep end. He went up to Leith with Captain Douglas, joined the ship in April 1978 and was immediately into the administration of the ship which now required the signing of articles, crew disbursements and victualling.

With the ship now in Leith undergoing the extensive alterations required by the DTI personnel were despatched to join the ship there. Captain Douglas was already standing by the vessel and the opportunity was taken for the new crew to familiarise themselves with the new ship prior to her entering service on 1st June. In the event they had longer to wait than anticipated.

Dave Egginson was one of the newly appointed First Officers and had joined the ship at Leith. He and others were working on the rear gantry on 13th June on the last day of his week on and almost a fortnight after the ship was supposed to be in service. Suddenly they noticed smoke billowing out of the ventilation ducts from the car deck. Realising the ship was on fire they made their way down to the car deck. There was no gangway to the dock and so the only way off for everyone was through the ship to the car deck which was smoke laden and over the stern ramp. It was because of this that crew and dockworkers were taken to Edinburgh hospital for respiratory checks. The relieving mate the following morning was Jack Woods who arrived at the dockyard to a scene of devastation and more work than he had bargained for!

Meanwhile, Guy Reid had set about establishing the office staff to start handling bookings and all the administration required for the enterprise as the bookings started to roll in for the projected TT sailings. Many of the office staff had come from the Tourist Board where Guy had previously worked. They were all young and keen and had a good knowledge of the Island and what it had to offer. From the outset the company introduced an airline-style ticketing system. This was

The ship's crew of the **Manx Viking** seen in the last days of operations.

revolutionary on Isle of Man sea routes and led to an easy integration with Sealink later who operated the TARS (ticket and reservation system).

When Geoff Duke's son Peter joined as Marketing Manager on 4th April 1978 he gave up a good job with excellent prospects in the motor industry to join the company. He was responsible for many innovative ideas.

Marketing carried numerous catchy strap lines. Although Manx Line was a Manx Company their efforts were concentrated on promoting the link from the UK, where most of the freight traffic was generated, via Heysham to the Isle of Man. The original sailing schedule was for four sailings within the 24-hour period Monday to Friday with five on Saturday and three on Sunday with a resulting high intensity of use for the ship. Attractive discounts were offered with 25% for senior citizens, 10% for students and 10% for organised groups. Special deals were offered to competitors in all the motorcycling and motor car events organised on the Island on proof of identity by their competition licence.

They continued to generate new business through innovative marketing and encouraged staff to put forward ideas. Day-trippers were catered for not just through the purchase of a day excursion ticket but by being sold the "Early Bird Mini-Cruise". It was a day trip by any other name except it had some extras! The ticket was for an out and back day trip from Douglas with no disembarkation at Heysham and was available any day of the week except Saturday. Departure was on the 07.00 sailing throughout the summer months with a fare of £8 for adults and £4 for children up to 14. It included a free bottle of wine on board and a £2 voucher to spend at the onboard shop.

"Early Bird One" was a long day trip by luxury coach to Hornsea Pottery and Blackpool with the same onboard benefits plus discount vouchers for Blackpool Pleasure Beach at a respective cost of £10.50 and £6. The trip was available only on Thursdays departing Douglas 07.00 and returning from Heysham at 23.00.

The last of the day trip excursions was marketed as "Early Bird Two". It was another long day excursion to Windermere via Hornsea Pottery and included a trip on Lake Windermere. The day ended with four hours in Morecambe and included reduced rates at the pleasure beach. The cost was £12.50 for adults and £7 for children.

One thing that became apparent was that many of those who had left the Steam Packet for the new company were either ignored in the street or in some cases verbally abused by their

The **Manx Viking** passing under the Erskine Bridge over the River Clyde on passage to Glasgow. (photo. Capt Ken Crellin collection)

former colleagues. This was particularly so with the navigating staff who were local and was to manifest itself again at the time of the merger, leading to acrimonious discussion at the meetings to determine staff integration.

The deck crew are not listed individually but they were drawn from the pool in Liverpool which was just about coming to an end as the means of engaging crew. Each crew had a Bosun and Quartermaster with eight Able Seamen divided into two watches with two on bridge duties and two on car deck and general duty, changing each trip.

During the first months of service the ship operated with two crews and the intensive working of the ship not only caused problems in the engineering department but also for the officers and crew.

Crew rostering was a headache for the First Officers and it took some time to arrive at a system that at least gave crew five hours of sleep in twenty-four! The officers too were feeling the strain because initially the ship was operating with crews on a one week on/one week off system which meant at least eight return trips per shift. It could not have been continued for much longer when the linkspan disaster occurred.

While the ship was at Harland & Wolff in Belfast following that incident the opportunity was taken to recruit more staff and reorganise the crewing arrangements so that, by the time she re-entered service, the three-crew system originally planned could to be put into operation. Crews worked two weeks on and one week off.

Catering was under the supervision of Shaun Orton who had been approached by Geoff Duke to join the company.

The manning levels for the start of the service in 1978 looked like this with commencement dates shown where known:-

MANX LINE LTD

Directors

J. Edmundson, G.E. Duke OBE, J. Counsell

SHIP MANNING 1978
SEAGOING STAFF

CAPT. R.M. DICKINSON	Master	24.04.78
CAPT. J.W. WOODS	Master	15.05.78
CAPT. T.K. CRELLIN	Master	21.05.78
D.EGGINSON	Chief Officer	
M.C.P. LEADLEY	Chief Officer	20.11.78
C.A. KNEALE	Chief/Second Officer	17.05.78
V.BOWE	Second Officer	03.04.78
H. BENSON	Radio Officer	07.05.78
K.GRATTON	Radio Officer	
M. PEAT	Chief Engineer	04.04.78
D. OLIVANT	Chief Engineer	04.05.78
J. MOLYNEAUX	Chief Engineer	15.05.78
F. O'NEILL	Second Engineer	01.06.78
R. LYON	Third Engineer	10.04.78
P. ODDIE	Third Engineer	09.09.78
A.KELLY	Eng Room CPO	05.78
P.WILKINSON	Eng Room PO	06.78
G.GREEN	Electrician	
J.GARRETT	Catering Officer	
J. KELLY	Catering Officer	30.08.78
G. QUINE	Purser	04.05.78
R. CATTERIL	Purser	06.78
J.BENJAMIN	Barman	

OFFICE PERSONNEL
ADMINISTRATIVE STAFF

G.REID	Office Manager	1977
P. G. DUKE	Marketing Manager	04.04.78
G. SHIMMIN	Personnel Manager	
S. D.ORTON	Catering Superintendent	
M. QUAYLE	Freight Operations Manager	
D. NOBLE	Freight Sales	

The increase in freight traffic also found the Freight Operations Manager Mike Quayle and his assistant D.Noble under pressure. The workload generating freight business was heavy enough but they were becoming snowed under with paper work. Import licences were required for livestock movements, including horses, for the UK Ministry of Agriculture and Fisheries. The Isle of Man legislation also required for example a licence for the importation of ice cream. The Road Traffic regulations in the Island were different from the UK and all of this was handled by the Freight Department. Tony Temple joined towards the end of 1979 to supplement the existing staff.

By the end of 1979 manning levels looked like this. The original staffing is shown in bold and the additional staff in lighter type:-

DIRECTORS

G.E. Duke

J.F.Hornby

G.Imlah

J.E.Crellin

C.Q.Savage

SHIP MANNING 1979
SEAGOING STAFF

CAPT. R.M. DICKINSON	Master	24.04.78
CAPT. J.W. WOODS	Master	15.05.78
CAPT. T.K. CRELLIN	Master	21.05.78
C.A. KNEALE	Chief Officer	17.05.78
M.C.P. LEADLEY	Chief Officer	20.11.78
R.E.MOORE	Chief Officer	24.05.79
V.BOWE	Second Officer	03.04.78
R.JACKSON	Second Officer	20.05.79
D.O'TOOLE	Second Officer	29.05.79
H. BENSON	Radio Officer	07.05.78
G.SMITH	Radio Officer	27.05.79
M. PEAT	Chief Engineer	04.04.78
D. OLIVANT	Chief Engineer	04.05.78
J. MOLYNEAUX	Chief Engineer	15.05.78
F. O'NEILL	Second Engineer	01.06.78
D.KELSO	Second Engineer	27.04.79
A.WESTRAN	Second Engineer	15.05.79
R. LYON	Third Engineer	10.04.78
P. ODDIE	Third Engineer	09.09.78
B.TRACEY	Third Engineer	27.04.79
T.ROBINSON	Third Engineer	27.06.79
M.GRIGLIN	Third Engineer	21.08.79
P.SMITH	Third Engineer	21.08.79
M.McLEOD	Electrician	06.79
E.FARGHER	Electrician	
J.MONTGOMERY	Electrician	
A.SANTAMARA	Chief Cook	
T.KEEFE	Chief Cook	
J. KELLY	Catering Officer	30.08.78
T.O'NEILL	Catering Officer	12.05.79
J.FITTON	Catering Officer	20.07.79
D.HOWELL	Asst.Catering Officer	12.05.79
D.DENARO	Asst. Catering Officer	18.05.79
C.McNULTY	Asst. Catering Officer	29.11.79
F.FEARON	Steward	
R.BARTON	Steward	
K.ELLIOTT	Steward	
J.BENJAMIN	Barman	
G.PATERSON	Barman	
P.SAILES	Asst.Barman	
G.QUINE	Purser	04.05.78
F.SMOKER	Purser	28.05.79
D.MERRICK	Purser	13.08.79
T.SANDLAND	Carpenter	
J.MALLON	Carpenter	
Marjorie HARDING	Hostess	
Penny MURRAY	Hostess	
Linda OWEN	Hostess	
Julie RUSSELL	Hostess	
Daphne RIDSDALE	Cashier	

OFFICE PERSONNEL
ADMINISTRATIVE STAFF

G.REID	Office Manager	1977
P.G.DUKE	Marketing Manager	04.04.78
G.SHIMMIN	Personnel Manager	
S.D.ORTON	Catering Superintendent	
M.QUAYLE	Freight Operations Manager	
D.NOBLE	Freight Sales	
T.TEMPLE	Freight Sales	09.79
P.LEWIN	Office Staff	
J.AINGE	Office Staff	
C.SMETHURST	Office Staff	
Ann ARTHUR	Office Staff	
Amber BRENNAN	Office Staff	
Sharon WILLIAMS	Office Staff	
C. ELLIS	Office Staff	

The Directors changed after the involvement of Fisher's in 1979:-

DIRECTORS

G.E.DUKE OBE
W. ECCLES
J.F.HORNBY
T. WM. CAIN
C.Q.SAVAGE

- and again in 1980 with the involvement of Sealink:-

G.E.DUKE OBE
J.F.HORNBY
G.IMLAH
J.E.CRELLIN
C.Q.SAVAGE

SEALINK/MANXLINE 1983
DIRECTORS

M.S.MILLER
CAPTAIN A.C.DOUGLAS
C.Q.SAVAGE

One of the rocks on which the company was founded was enthusiasm and this was reflected in the intense loyalty of the early employees throughout the life of the company.

Ironically two decades on many of the personnel from Manx Line who rejoined their old company at the time of the merger were to end up with senior positions in the Isle of Man Steam Packet Company.

Chapter 7 - Memorabilia

The final collection of publicity and advertising material shows how progressive Manx Line were at promoting the new service and each page needs little in the way of explanation being largely self explanatory.

Each page gives an interesting insight into the way the company targeted specific markets. Some of the marketing was particularly aggressive and much was directed at the lucrative motorcycling market. Great use was made of Geoff Duke's reputation as a former world motorcycling champion in the campaign and as you will see it was cleverly executed.

The material is just a small selection from the huge amount gathered from the personal collections of Peter Duke, Ken Crellin, Frank O'Neill and Tony Temple for which I am very much indebted.

A number of car and motorcycle stickers were produced, one in particular laying emphasis on the fact that Manx Line did not require motorcycle fuel tanks to be emptied for travel to the Isle of Man as was the case with the Steam Packet which did not have special facilities for securing bikes. The Isle of Man resident was not neglected and free car stickers with the GBM international circulation plate carrying the Manx Line logo were issued with their ticketing to all vehicles leaving the Island for travel to the UK or the Continent.

In the High Court of Justice

QUEEN'S BENCH DIVISION
ADMIRALTY COURT
LIVERPOOL   **District Registry**

1978— T.—No. 3652

ADMIRALTY action in rem against :

Admiralty 1A

Writ of Summons
in Admiralty Action
in Rem
(*District Registry*)
(O.75, r. 3)

Oyez Publishing
Limited
Norwich House
11/13 Norwich Street
London EC4A 1AB
a subsidiary of
The Solicitors'
Law Stationery Society,
Limited

F23603. 3/77

★ ★ ★ ★

(1) Or as may be
describing the res.

(2) The Owners of
the Ship "Y" or as
may be.

(3) The Ship "X"
or as may be
describing the res.

(4) Or Cargo, &c., as
may be.

The Ship(¹)   "MANX VIKING"
(²)

TRITEC MARITIME LIMITED   **PLAINTIFFS**

AND

The Owners of(³)

THE MOTOR VESSEL "MANX VIKING"
   DEFENDANTS

Elizabeth the Second, by the Grace of God, of the United Kingdom of Great Britain and Northern Ireland and of Our other realms and territories Queen, Head of the Commonwealth, Defender of the Faith : To the [Owners of and other] persons interested in the Ship

"MANX VIKING"

of the Port of   DOUGLAS, ISLE OF MAN
(⁴)

WE COMMAND YOU that within 14 days after the service of this Writ, inclusive of the day of service, you do cause an appearance to be entered for you in an action at the suit of

TRITEC MARITIME LIMITED   ;

and take notice that in default of your so doing the Plaintiffs may proceed therein, and judgment may be given in your absence, and if the res described in this Writ is then under arrest of the Court it may be sold by order of the Court.

Witness, FREDERICK BARON ELWYN JONES

Lord High Chancellor of Great Britain,

the   17th   day of   OCTOBER,   , 19 78.

NOTE.—This Writ may not be served later than 12 calendar months beginning with the above date unless renewed by order of the Court.

DIRECTIONS FOR ENTERING APPEARANCE

If the Defendants reside or carry on business, or (in the case of a limited company) have a registered office, within the district of the above-named District Registry or the Writ is indorsed with a statement that any cause of action in respect of which the Plaintiffs claim relief wholly or in part arose in that district, the Defendants must enter an appearance in person or by a Solicitor in the District Registry and may do so either (1) by handing in the appropriate forms, duly completed,

* Insert address of office.

at the office of the District Registrar,*   4th Floor, India Buildings, Water Street, Liverpool   or (2) by sending them to that office by post.

If the Defendants neither reside nor carry on business nor (in the case of a limited company) have a registered office within the district of the above-named District Registry and the Writ is not indorsed with a statement that any cause of action in respect of which the Plaintiffs claim relief wholly or in part arose in that district, the Defendants may enter an appearance in person or by a Solicitor either (1) by handing in the appropriate forms, duly completed, at the office of the District Registrar, or by sending them to that office by post, or (2) by handing in the said forms, duly completed, at the Admiralty Registry, Royal Courts of Justice, Strand, London WC2A 2LL, or by sending them to that office by post.

† Insert address of District Registry.

The appropriate forms may be obtained by sending a postal order for 14p with an addressed envelope, foolscap size, to (1) the District Registrar, High Court of Justice, † 4th Floor, India Buildings, Water Street, Liverpool   if the appearance is to be entered in the District Registry, or (2) The Clerk of Accounts, Vote Office, Royal Courts of Justice, Strand, London WC2A 2LL, if the appearance is to be entered in London.

This is one of several writs served on the vessel during the first year of operation when Manx Line were cash-strapped following the refunds which had to be made due to the late delivery from the shipyard in 1978. The problem were only solved by the intervention of James Fishers & Sons and Sealink.

UK MAINLAND – ISLE-OF-MAN

ROLL-ON-ROLL-OFF SERVICE

Introducing a brand new service – setting a new, high standard . . . . .

Commencing service in early 1978, Manx Line's Roll-on-Roll-off 'super-ship' Manx Viking heralds the start of a new era of transport between the UK Mainland and the Isle-of-Man.

Operating between Heysham and Douglas, the 2700 ton ferry carries up to 260 vehicles – while passengers start their holidays in the air-conditioned luxury of the comfortable lounges, self-service restaurant and fully licensed bars.

With Heysham just 8 miles from the M6 motorway, ample car parking and a British Rail terminal virtually on-board the ship, there's never been a more convenient way to travel.

Just 'roll-on' at Heysham and 'roll-off' at Douglas – with no fuss, no long delays.

Manx Line offer a minimum of 3 crossings every day and this leaflet gives full details of sailing schedules and fares, plus the many special rates and discount schemes available.

So whether you're travelling for business or pleasure make it Manx Line – the modern way from the Mainland to Man.

Manx Line's 2,700 ton, 260 car, Manx Viking.

UK MAINLAND – ISLE-OF-MAN

ROLL-ON-ROLL-OFF SERVICE

From Heysham to Douglas – to make life easier for you . . .

Heysham is just 8 miles from the M6 motorway – giving quick and easy access to and from most major towns in the UK.

A 'ship-side' British Rail terminal links up with main-line routes to all parts of the UK.

GENERAL INFORMATION

ADVANCE BOOKING
Early advanced booking is advisable for both outward and return journeys.

GROUPS
Special group rates are available for parties of 10 or more. Please ask for details.

SENIOR CITIZENS 25% DISCOUNT
On normal single fares when booked in advance. (except Friday and Saturday sailings from 1st June to 31st August)
ELIGIBILITY
(a) Gentlemen 65 years and over
(b) Ladies 60 years and over on production of Pension Book
(c) Married couples – At least one person to qualify under category (a) or (b).

STUDENTS 10% DISCOUNT
On normal single fares when booked in advance and N.U.S. card shown. (except Friday and Saturday sailings from 1st June to 31st August)

PETROL
Do not overfill your petrol tank. Petrol containers must not be carried.

GAS
Gas cylinders may be carried, but must be turned off – and properly sealed. This also applies to fridges in motorised caravans.

DEPARTURE
It is essential for vehicles to arrive at the departure dock not less than 30 minutes before scheduled sailing time.

VEHICLE LENGTH
Overall length of vehicle means either the length from bumper to bumper as shown in the manufacturer's specification or the actual length (including trailers and fixed towbars on cars) – whichever is the greater.
Bumpers and overriders should not be removed.

TWO DAY RETURN
The 'Two Day Return' is available for travel out on specified days for return on the same or following day.

SHORT STAY RETURN
The 'Short Stay Return' is available for travel between 1st June and 31st August. The outward journey to be made any day Sunday to Wednesday inclusive, with the return journey during the same week Tuesday to Friday.

MOTORISTS BARGAINS
The 'Two Day Return' and 'Short Stay Return' are timed as detailed above.

CARAVANS
Please note: Towed caravans are not permitted on the Isle-of-Man.

N.B. The information given in this leaflet is to the best of the publisher's knowledge, correct at the time of going to press, but is subject to alteration.
The company reserves the right to alter prices and sailing times without prior notice.

BOOKING FORM (CONTINUED)

SLEEPING ACCOMMODATION AND DAY CABINS.
Exclusive use of cabin is possible if the occupier pays for both berths in that cabin.

2 Berth Cabin required Delete as required *	OUTWARD		RETURN	
	Night/Day*		Night/Day*	
Single Berth only required (ie. sharing 2 berth cabin)	MALE	FEMALE	MALE	FEMALE
Reserved seat with rug. (state No. required) Night sailings only 24.00 to 06.00				

NB: Sleeping accommodation on night sailings is limited.

VEHICLE	MAKE:
Model	Year	Reg. No.

Overall length of vehicle or vehicle and trailer (including roof-top luggage)

Motorcycle Reg. No.   Solo/Combination (delete as required)

Cycle (state quantity)

TERMS AND CONDITIONS
Tickets are issued on the Carrier's terms and conditions which contain exclusions of and/or restrictions on the carriers liability for death, illness or injury or for damage to or loss of vehicles and/or baggage. Copies of the terms and conditions are available at the carrier's offices and will be supplied on request.

UK MAINLAND – ISLE-OF-MAN

ROLL-ON-ROLL-OFF SERVICE

1978 FARES HEYSHAM TO DOUGLAS

All rates and fares shown are for single journeys unless otherwise stated.
To calculate return fares and rates add together the single fares shown for the two dates upon which you will be travelling.
Fares for each single journey are charged at the seasonal rate applicable to the date of travel.

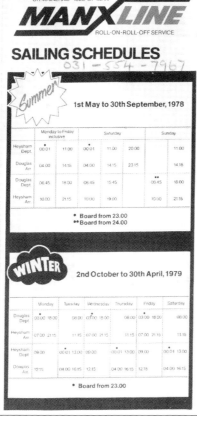

UK MAINLAND – ISLE-OF-MAN

ROLL-ON-ROLL-OFF SERVICE

SAILING SCHEDULES

031 – 554 – 7967

Summer 1st May to 30th September, 1978

	Monday to Friday inclusive		Saturday			Sunday	
Heysham Dept.	00.01	11.00	00.01	11.00	20.00		11.00
Douglas Arr.	04.00	14.15	04.00	14.15	23.15		14.15
Douglas Dept.	06.45	18.00	06.45	15.45		06.45	18.00
Heysham Arr.	10.00	21.15	10.00	19.00		10.00	21.15

* Board from 23.00
** Board from 24.00

Winter 2nd October to 30th April, 1979

	Monday	Tuesday	Wednesday	Thursday	Friday	Saturday
Douglas Dept.	08.00 18.00		08.00 18.00		08.00 18.00	08.00
Heysham Arr.	07.00 21.15		11.15 07.00 21.15		11.15 07.00 21.15	11.15
Heysham Dept.	09.00	00.01 13.00	09.00	00.01 13.00	09.00	00.01 13.00
Douglas Arr.	12.15	04.00 16.15	12.15	04.00 16.15	12.15	04.00 16.15

* Board from 23.00

UK MAINLAND – ISLE-OF-MAN

ROLL-ON-ROLL-OFF SERVICE

Roll-on-Roll-off service – UK Mainland to Isle-of-Man.

The first brochure issued by the company in 1978 was a modest affair but already was offering cheaper fares than the Isle of Man Steam Packet with whom of course they were in direct competition.

MANX LINE

The only Roll-on-Roll-off car ferry to the Isle of Man

Heysham to Douglas/Summer 1979
1st May to 30th September

With Fisher's and Sealink now in the frame the 1979 brochure was a much more ambitious affair set at promoting the new ro-ro service to the Isle of Man.

First for comfort because you come first . . . .

Manx Viking doesn't just give you a new way of travelling to the Isle of Man, she sets a new high standard of passenger comfort too.

In fact, everything about Manx Viking is geared to make your journey a pleasure – from the moment you step aboard, you come first.

How? Just take a look at Manx Viking's many 'comfort-plus' features.

First with air-conditioning

All the passenger areas aboard Manx Viking have full, temperature controlled air-conditioning – so you're never too hot or too cold and never subjected to a stale, smoke-filled atmosphere.

Manx Viking is also fully stabilised, to keep you on an even keel even when the Irish Sea lives up to its worst reputation.

First-class self-service restaurant

Situated centrally on the main passenger deck, the King Harald Restaurant offers the very best in modern, self-service catering.

The spacious restaurant, named after one of the Island's Viking kings, can accommodate 150 people in a pleasant, relaxing atmosphere and offers a wide menu of tasty snacks, meals and beverages – with generous helpings and really reasonable prices. Special portions, at reduced prices, are available for children.

First with a comfortable seat for everyone

'Luxury seating' hardly describes the sumptuous, Spanish leather, aircraft-type seating aboard Manx Viking.

And, what's more, there are plenty of them. More than 260 situated forward in the quiet, relaxing King Olaf lounge, with its special non-smoking area.

And almost 300 of them in the King Ivar video lounge situated further aft on the passenger deck.

Then, in addition to the aircraft type seating there is further seating in the King Magnus bar and, of course, seating for 150 in the restaurant.

All of which add up to a seat for every one of Manx Viking's 750 passengers.

First to accept full size caravanettes and motorised caravans

If you own one of the larger motorised caravans you can now add the Isle of Man to your list of ideal holidays.

Manx Viking can accept any road-legal vehicles up to 4.3 metres (14') high, and there's no limit on length either, provided you comply with Manx law.

Remember TOWED caravans are not permitted on the Island's roads.

First to put you in the holiday mood

Whatever your idea of relaxing surroundings, Manx Viking has the answer.

For those who prefer to sit and enjoy the smoothest, quietest trip possible, there's the King Olaf lounge, with its special 'no-smoking' section. Situated to the front of the ship, this is the ideal place to while away a pleasant, relaxing journey.

If however you prefer something a little more lively, then just head upstairs to the rear of the ship and the main King Magnus bar – complete with its dance floor and doors opening onto the adjoining sun-deck – this is the ideal place to show-off your best steps or, weather permitting, to make a start on that holiday tan.

Or, if you'd like something lively but not too energetic (or you'd like to keep the kids amused) then this is for you . . .

First with big-screen video

. . . situated to the aft of the passenger deck is the 292 seat, King Ivar lounge, with its adjoining bar and full-colour, big-screen video TV system.

The lounge has 3 screens in all, and features a wide variety of up-to-the-minute cinema, T.V. and 'special interest' films.

Inside the 1979 brochure much was made of the comfortable seating, the video entertainment and onboard facilities and the special arrangements for transporting motorcycles using specially designed racks.

The 1980 brochures continued to promote the concept of ro-ro to the Isle of Man as the modern way to travel and were directed principally at the UK customer.

MANX LINE

The modern way to the Isle of Man...

When the Manx Line ferry service was introduced in 1978, it represented not just an alternative link between the UK mainland and the Isle of Man, but, most important, it also marked the introduction of a really modern 'cross-channel' type service.

If you've ever taken your car to the continent, you'll know just how quick and easy it is – with the opening bow and stern doors allowing you to simply 'drive through' the ship.

Well, Manx Line's 2700 ton ferry Manx Viking is the only Isle of Man car ferry offering exactly the same facility.

Sailing from conveniently situated Heysham, Lancashire twice daily throughout the summer and 10 times per week in winter, Manx Viking operates on a new short route to Douglas, the Isle of Man's capital, offering an approximate crossing time of just 3¾ hours.

Manx Viking can carry up to 200 cars per crossing and, as you'll see from this brochure, the 'drive-through' facility is just one of the many 'up-to-the-minute' features you'll find aboard the Isle of Man's most modern ferry – all of them designed to make your journey a pleasure.

And, in case you think all this is bound to cost you more, then the price list in this brochure should come as a pleasant surprise.

So, compare what you get, compare what it costs, and we think you'll agree Manx Line give you so much more for your money.

Welcome aboard!

The inside cover of the 1980 brochure continued the "modern way to travel to the Isle of Man" theme and emphasized how quick and easy it was to drive on and off the ship.

Heysham-Douglas

Sealink **Isle of Man**

From 10th October 1980 the Heysham-Douglas service was marketed under the Sealink/Isle of Man banner and the 1981 brochure was produced in the same manner.

The company valued its motorcycle business and fought to win a large share of this lucrative traffic visiting the Island for the TT and MGP events. Extensive advertising campaigns were launched in the trade and motorcycling press using Geoff Duke's association with the sport and the company to advantage.

Ride our new MV to the Isle of Man for as little as £9.50.

We'd like to introduce you to Manx Line's new 'super ferry' MV Manx Viking.

She's not quite as quick as the MV you might expect to read about in your favourite bike magazine, but she's still packed with a whole lot of good things to interest bikers bound for the Isle of Man.

Because Manx Viking heralds the start of the island's first roll-on-roll-off service and operates on a new, quick route between Heysham and Douglas.

The modern 2,700 ton vessel is fully stabilised and air-conditioned and offers luxury accommodation with air-craft type seating, 2 licensed bars, a comfortable, self-service restaurant and a 'big-screen' TV lounge with up-to-the-minute movies and bike racing films.

Prices start as low as just £9.50 for a single fare Monday to Thursday.

So if you're going to the Manx Grand Prix or Two Day Trial, why not ride our new MV, and while you're being looked after upstairs, your bike is safe and secure below decks in the purpose built motor cycle racks with 8000lb breaking strain restraining straps.

Write to Manx Line Limited, Douglas, Isle of Man or ask at your local travel agent.

IMPORTANT NOTICE

Many of you will have heard about, or experienced at first hand, our unfortunate last minute cancellation of bookings for the TT.

This was entirely due to Manx Viking's refit being delayed by problems in the shipyard and was totally outside Manx Line's control.

Please rest assured that Manx Viking is now fully operational and you may book in complete confidence.

Passengers for the Grand Prix or Two Day Trial who had a cancelled booking in TT week will, of course, be entitled to a FREE booking.

MANX LINE'S
RO-RO VESSEL
MV MANX VIKING

MANX LINE

Manx Line Limited, UK Mainland to Isle of Man Roll-on-Roll-off service.

Continuing the same theme this whole page advert played on the 'double entendre' of MV - alluding to the MV Agusta motorcycle and the MV **Manx Viking.**

More on the same theme - this delightful and amusing cartoon was geared to the Continental motorcycle fraternity who visited the Island in large numbers for these events.

ROCKERS SPECIALS

Inclusive Packages to the Isle of Man
1980 Rock 'n Roll Festival

14th to 20th September, 1980
At Summerland, Douglas, Isle of Man

Visitors to the Isle of Man Rock and Roll Festival in 1980 were offered inclusive packages embracing travel, accommodation and entrance fees.

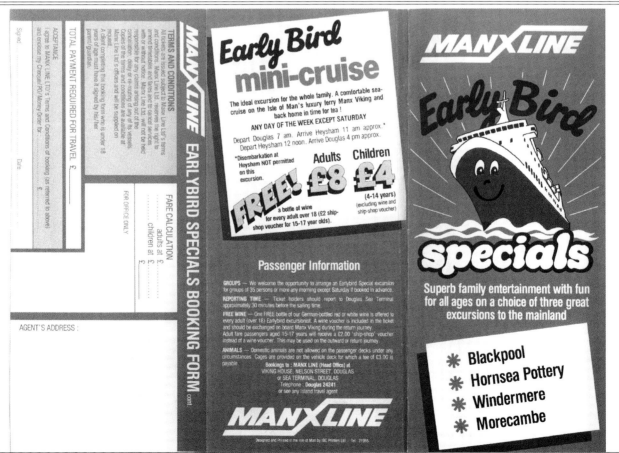

1980 was a pivotal year for the company which was now part of the North West Sealink group and using this new connection came up with the 'Early Bird Specials' which aimed at generating mid-week traffic. They proved popular with Island residents.

Isle of Man Ro-Ro means better business for you.

Now, driver and vehicle can go all the way – with less risk, less cost, less delay.

As a transport operator, you won't need us to tell you the many benefits of roll-on-roll-off freight shipping.

Ro-ro services have long been established on many major freight-routes and the system has gained wide acceptance as the really cost-effective method of achieving quick delivery with maximum security.

For several years there was on-going discussion regarding the possible introduction of such a service between the Isle of Man and the UK mainland.

However, no action resulted from these discussions and this important link continued to use slow, cumbersome 'lifting' methods of freight handling – and transport companies continued to suffer all the restrictions imposed by such systems.

Then, two years ago, we appeared on the scene. We're a modern, go-ahead, Manx shipping company, called, aptly enough, Manx Line.

And, while the others have been talking, we've been busy.

We've built a brand-new, metal 'linkspan' roadway in Douglas harbour.

We've located the ideal UK mainland port – Heysham, Lancashire.

MV. MANX VIKING ENTERING DOUGLAS HARBOUR.

It's open and accessible and just 8 miles from the M6 motorway.

We've bought a modern, multi-million pound ferry with opening bow and stern doors.

And we've gone right ahead and introduced the Isle of Man's first ever drive through ro-ro service – opening up a whole new era in freight transport both to and from the island.

Just think of the possibilities . . . Fresh Manx scallops to France and Belgium . . .

Oven-fresh cereals to Manx supermarkets . . .

Same-day delivery of just about anything you care to name!

All thanks to Manx Line.

Let's take a closer look at what our service has to offer.

Both Pages 66/67: Not so often seen are some of the promotional efforts in respect of freight traffic. Here is one of the freight brochures directed at delivery services to and from the Isle of Man which was the main business on which Manx Line was built and which so seriously affected the Steam Packet Company.

Manx Line Ro-Ro. Better for operators, better for drivers, better for business.

Our ship, Manx Viking, is 2,700 tons of fast, modern ferry with easy 'drive-through' vehicle access, big, roomy vehicle decks and a super-efficient stabilisation system to ensure a smooth ride – even in the roughest of conditions!

And, if your vehicles are well looked after, your drivers are positively pampered. The upper decks feature just about everything

LUXURY SEATING FOR EVERYONE.

they could need to turn their journey into a pleasant, relaxing break.

There's a modern, self-service restaurant offering a wide range of tasty snacks, hot meals and beverages.

Licensed bars and a 3-screen video TV lounge with a variety of film entertainment.

There's a shop and vending machines.

Plenty of deeply-padded armchair-type seats.

And, last but not least, full, temperature-controlled air conditioning – so the passenger areas are never too hot or too cold and there's never a stale, smoke or fuel-filled atmosphere.

Our UK port, Heysham, offers ample parking and easy access and is ideally located for all points in the UK including, of course, the Channel ports.

Our Isle of Man port is Douglas, the island's capital, where our

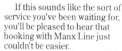

modern harbour facilities ensure quick loading and unloading of even the largest vehicles (max 13ms. articulated allowed by Manx law).

If this sounds like the sort of service you've been waiting for, you'll be pleased to hear that booking with Manx Line just couldn't be easier.

Inside this brochure you'll find all you need to know about bookings, regulations, licensing requirements, and so on.

If you have any further queries or wish to make a booking, simply contact Manx Line on Heysham (0524) 53802, Telex: 65260, and ask for 'Freight'.

SEE INSIDE FOR FULL INFORMATION, MANX REGULATIONS, ETC.

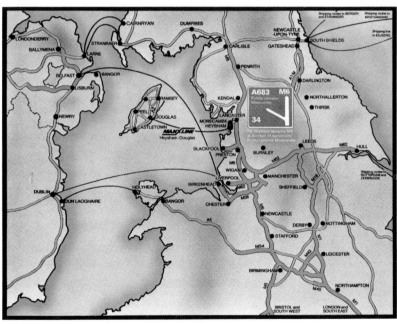
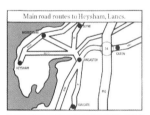

Manx Line Ltd, The Harbour, Heysham, Lancashire.
Telephone: Heysham (0524) 53802.
Sea Terminal, Douglas, Isle of Man.
Tel: Douglas (0624) 24241. Telex: 628517. Viking G.

ISLE OF MAN RO-RO SERVICE

Printed in the Isle of Man by Print Centres Limited

No. Name of Ship, Port of Registry, Official No. and Gross or Register Tonnage	Date and place of Joining ship	Date and place of Leaving ship	Capacity	No. Description of voyage	Signature of Master or an authorised person	Official or Company Stamp
1 OFF No 359765 DOUGLAS G.T. 2752.63 BHP 8400	28.5.79 DOUGLAS	8.11.79 DOUGLAS	ASST PURSER	1 H/T PASS.	[signature]	MANX VIKING OFF No 359765 DOUGLAS G.T. 2752.63 BHP 8400
2 MANX VIKING OFF No 359765 DOUGLAS MANX VIKING BHP 8400	6/12/79 DOUGLAS	28.11.80 DOUGLAS	ASST PURSER	2 H/T PASS	[signature]	MANX VIKING OFF No 359765 DOUGLAS G.T. 2752.63 BHP 8400
3 OFF No 359 DOUGLAS G.T. 2752.63 BHP 8400	29/11/80	29.5.80 HEYSHAM	ASST PURSER	3 H/T PASS	[signature]	MANX VIKING OFF No 359765 DOUGLAS
4 MANX VIKING OFF No 359765 DOUGLAS G.T. 2752.63 BHP 8400	29.5.80 HEYSHAM	8.12.80 BELFAST	ASST PURSER	4 H/T PASS	[signature] -8 DEC 1980 BELFAST	MANX VIKING OFF No 359765 DOUGLAS
5 MANX VIKING OFF No 359765 DOUGLAS G.T. 2752.63 BHP 8400	9.12.80 BELFAST	25.3.81 HEYSHAM	ASST PURSER	5 H.T PASS	Rmdurrmson	MANX VIKING OFF No 359765 DOUGLAS G.T. 2752.63 BHP 8400
6 M.V. EARL GODWIN LONDON O.N. 363678 G.R.T. 3776.88 N.R.T. 1866.61	25/3/81 Heysham	2.4.81 Heysham	A/Purser	6 H.T	S Crumet	SEALINK U.K. LTD EVERSHOLT HOUSE LONDON NW1 1BG

Finally two pages from the discharge book of Purser Geoff Quine which make for interesting reading, providing an insight into the various locations of vessels at times of signing on and off.

No. Name of Ship, Port of Registry, Official No. and Gross or Register Tonnage	Date and place of Joining ship	Date and place of Leaving ship	Capacity	No. Description of voyage	Signature of Master or an authorised person	Official or Company Stamp
13 AILSA PRINCESS ON 341458. LONDON.	24/2/83 DOUGLAS	4/3/83 DOUGLAS	ASST PURSER	13 H/T PASS.	[signature]	AILSA PRINCESS
14 m.v. MANX VIKING DOUGLAS I.O.M. OFFICIAL No. 359765 GT 3589.43 BHP 8400	5/3/83 DOUGLAS	11/5/83 DOUGLAS	ASST PURSER	14 H/T PASS	[signature]	m.v. MANX VIKING DOUGLAS I.O.M. OFFICIAL No. 359765 GT 3589.43 BHP 8400
15 m.v. MANX VIKING DOUGLAS I.O.M. OFFICIAL No. 359765 GT 3589.43 BHP 8400	12/5/83 DOUGLAS	22/6/83 DOUGLAS	ASST PURSER	15 H/T PASS	[signature]	m.v. MANX VIKING DOUGLAS I.O.M. OFFICIAL No. 359765 GT 3589.43 BHP 8400
16 VILLANDRY DIEPPE O/N 3525	23/6/83 DOVER	6/7/83 DOUGLAS	ASST PURSER	16 H/T PASS.	[signature]	VILLANDRY
17 m.v. MANX VIKING DOUGLAS I.O.M. OFFICIAL No. 359765 GT 3589.43 BHP 8400	10/7/83 DOUGLAS	16/11/83 Douglas	ASST PURSER	17 H/T PASS.	[signature]	m.v. MANX VIKING DOUGLAS I.O.M. OFFICIAL No. 359765 GT 3589.43 BHP 8400
18 m.v. MANX VIKING DOUGLAS I.O.M. OFFICIAL No. 359765 GT 3589.43 BHP 8400	17/11/83 DOUGLAS	16/5/84 DOUGLAS	ASST PURSER	18 H/T PASS	[signature]	m.v. MANX VIKING DOUGLAS I.O.M. OFFICIAL No. 359765 GT 3589.43 BHP 8400

Sail Sealink to the
ISLE OF MAN

1981

Sealink
Isle of Man
Heysham–Douglas

The **Manx Viking** in Sealink livery departs from Douglas in a north-easterly gale.

APPENDIX ONE
THE SHIPS

Red Star Shipping
mv Zwaluw
mv Reiger

Ronagency (Shipping) Ltd.
mv LIRECO
mv CAPACITY
mv PAVONIS
mv ANTARCTICA
mv CON ZELO
mv A.HELD
mv MERIZELL
mv GLORIA
mv ALDERD L
mv KON TIKI
mv NORTHGATE
mv SUSANNE SCAN
mv TOWER DUCHESS
mv ROYALGATE
mv KINGSGATE
mv TOWER ENTERPRISE
mv TOWER MARIE
mv PARKESGATE
mv HEATHERGATE
mv WELLOWGATE (Susanne Scan)
mv WIS
mv WIB
mv CELEBRITY

Manx Line Ltd
mv MANX VIKING (Monte Castillo)
mv CELEBRITY
mv EDEN FISHER
mv POOL FISHER
mv DALRIADA
mv LAGAN BRIDGE
mv LUNE BRIDGE
mv VIKING III
mv ANTRIM PRINCESS
mv EARL GODWIN
mv VIKING VICTORY
mv AILSA PRINCESS
mv VILLANDRY

Acknowledgements

This story would not have been possible without the help I have received from many people who were directly involved and even now after the passage of time their enthusiasm for the company which was to speed the change of sea travel to and from the Isle of Man still comes through. The huge personal commitment that many of the seafarers took with young families to give up what must have seemed like a secure job says much for their character and the support of their families.

I am particularly indebted to Bob Dearden and Geoff Duke who gave me encouragement when I started this in 1999. To John Edmundson, William Cain, Colin Savage, Peter Duke, Captain Andrew Douglas, Captain Ken Crellin, Captain Roger Moore, Captain Jack Woods, Dave Egginson, Captain Dermot O'Toole, Captain. Michael Brew, Frank O'Neill, Shaun Orton, Tony Temple, Geoff Quine, Brian Kennedy, David Parsons and Charlie Coole a big thank you for help and memories freely given. Thanks as always to Roger Sims and his staff at the Manx Museum for their help.

Miles Cowsill and John Hendy of Ferry Publications are also thanked for their support in both editing my manuscript and helping to bring the book to fruition. Without their assistance, the book would never have been published.

Most of the photographs were taken by me but my special thanks for photographs and memorabilia supplied from the personal collections of those mentioned above and acknowledged within the book where appropriate.

The **Manx Viking** at Douglas.